C0-AKR-558

THE GREAT AMERICAN THINKERS SERIES

This series of original works is designed to present in highly readable form the flow of American thought from colonial times to the present. Each volume has been written by a leading scholar and is devoted to a single man in the history of American thought who represents a particular trend or movement within the great span of our culture. Each book in the series contains a short biography of the man, a critical evaluation of his central ideas and their influence upon American thought as a whole, as well as an extensive bibliography and an index.

The Great American Thinkers Series is under the general editorship of two distinguished American educators: Dr. Arthur W. Brown, Dean of the Graduate School of Arts and Sciences at Fordham University and past President of Adelphi University, and Dr. Thomas S. Knight, Professor and Chairman of the Department of Philosophy at Adelphi University. *George Santayana* was written by Dr. Willard E. Arnett, Chairman of the Department of Philosophy at Chatham College, Pittsburgh, Pennsylvania.

☆

The GREAT AMERICAN THINKERS *Series*

JONATHAN EDWARDS • *Alfred Owen Aldridge*
BENJAMIN FRANKLIN • *Ralph L. Ketcham*
JOHN WOOLMAN • *Edwin H. Cady*
THOMAS JEFFERSON • *Stuart Gerry Brown*
JOHN C. CALHOUN • *Richard N. Current*
GEORGE BANCROFT • *Russel B. Nye*
CHAUNCEY WRIGHT • *Edward H. Madden*
CHARLES PEIRCE • *Thomas S. Knight*
WILLIAM JAMES • *Edward C. Moore*
THORSTEIN VEBLEN • *Douglas F. Dowd*
JOHN DEWEY • *Richard J. Bernstein*
ALEXANDER HAMILTON • *Stuart Gerry Brown*
JOSIAH ROYCE • *Thomas F. Powell*
GEORGE SANTAYANA • *Willard E. Arnett*

IN PREPARATION

JAMES MADISON • *Neal Riemer*
RALPH WALDO EMERSON • *Warren Staebler*
THEODORE PARKER • *Arthur W. Brown*
THEODORE ROOSEVELT • *William Harbaugh*
ALFRED NORTH WHITEHEAD • *Nathaniel Lawrence*
DR. W. E. B. DU BOIS • *Henry Lee Moon*
NORMAN THOMAS • *Robert J. Alexander*
HENRY DAVID THOREAU • *James G. Murray*

GEORGE SANTAYANA

Author of this volume: Willard E. Arnett, Ph.D., Chairman of the Department of Philosophy, Chatham College.

Series Editors: Arthur W. Brown, Ph.D., Dean of the Graduate School, Fordham University; and Thomas S. Knight, Ph.D., Professor and Chairman of the Department of Philosophy, Adelphi University.

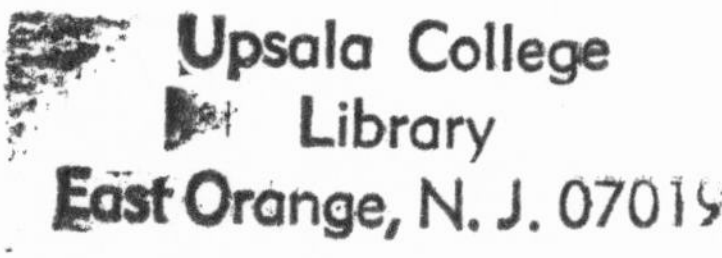

Twayne Publishers, Inc. :: New York

To LESLEY RUTH

This Twayne Publishers edition
is published by special arrangement with
Washington Square Press, Inc.

 Printed in the U.S.A.

PREFACE

No system of philosophic thought is more vulnerable to critical or logical analysis than that of George Santayana. He often contradicted himself and sometimes defended claims that were profoundly dubious and paradoxical. Yet the seriousness as well as the style and scope of his works places him clearly among the most provocative thinkers of the twentieth century. His imagination was unusually fertile and his sense for the humanly important highly reliable. He thus provides an important and stimulating, if somewhat unorthodox and questionable, approach to the basic aims, problems, and values of philosophy. Accordingly I have tried to make of this book not only an introduction to the life and thought of George Santayana but also an introduction to some of the central problems of philosophy, particularly as such problems have been formulated by recent American thinkers.

Certain persons have contributed in very important ways to the completion of this book. My wife, Patricia, besides suggesting changes that have made it more readable, has done more than a wife can reasonably be expected to do to make it possible for me to study and write without serious interruptions; Pamela E. Johnson has worked diligently and carefully to make the footnotes and bibliography as accurate as possible; a very special note of gratitude is due, however, to Professor John A. Lester, Jr., of Haverford College, who so graciously shared his study in the woods by the beautiful Tusket River in Nova Scotia where most of these pages were written and rewritten; his interest, questions, and comments, as well as the very atmosphere of the place, made the conditions of work as nearly ideal as is possible.

W. E. A. Pittsburgh, Pennsylvania

☆

CONTENTS

Chapter 1

INTRODUCTION

"... I have been looking for the high lights that here and there, in various directions, might shine in the revolutions of nature and of history."

"Apologia Pro Mente Sua"

George Santayana, it is now sometimes claimed, was neither an "American" nor a "great thinker" or philosopher. And it is of course true that he was born in Spain of Spanish parents and lived there, knowing no language except Spanish, until he was nine years old; furthermore, as both student and professor at Harvard he traveled and lived in Europe at every opportunity. He never became an American citizen; and he spent the last forty years of his life largely in England, Spain, and Italy without a single visit to the United States. He also said of himself in one of his later works that he was not an American, "except by long association," though he admitted on the very next page that, "After all, it has been acquaintance with America and American philosophers that has chiefly contributed to clear and settle my own mind."[1] Although there are then indeed certain "ironies," to use the word Philip B. Rice used in a similar context in 1951,[2] attached to the inclusion of Santayana in a series on "great American thinkers," it is also true and no less important that he received most of his philosophical education at Harvard under the direction of William James and Josiah Royce, who are certainly among the most influential "American thinkers." His American friends, he said, were "more numerous, more loyal, more sympathetic, and with two or three exceptions more beloved than my friends of other nationalities." The manners and tastes of Americans, he added, were "more natural to me than any others."[3]

And also only in America has he had significant influence as both a man of letters and a philosopher. Although this influence has not been wide or deep even in America, particularly if one counts only the philosophical papers and scholarly books which his work has inspired or influenced, nonetheless several distinguished thinkers and an uncounted number of sensitive and intelligent readers have either been influenced by or found much to applaud in the thought as well as in the extraordinary grace and style of his many books. He was at the very least an unusually reflective mind with an extraordinary gift for the most felicitous use of language. No doubt he spoke truly of himself when he said late in life, "My intellectual relations and labours still unite me closely to America; and it is as an American writer that I must be counted if I am counted at all."[4] Although the future may decide not to count him at all, only ignorance or prejudice can now exclude him from the list of distinguished American thinkers.

Yet in a recent volume on *The Spirit of American Philosophy* Santayána was dismissed in the preface with the claim that "despite his presence in the 'golden age' of American philosophy his thought is not representative of the main drift of American thinking." John E. Smith, the author of this questionable and largely irrelevant claim, was of course unable to indicate just what the "main drift" of American thought is, though he did assert that the American mind is "voluntaristic and not contemplative," "moral and moralistic rather than aesthetic," religious rather than poetic, and committed to views that assert rather than deny the ultimate reality of the self. Thus, according to Smith, "The American mind . . . has been everything but what Santayana was and stood for."[5]

Now apart from the dubious assumption that there is a "main drift of American thinking" or a characteristically American turn of mind typified by C. S. Peirce, William James, Josiah Royce, John Dewey, and A. N. Whitehead, this summary dismissal is altogether unfair not only to Santayana but especially to the great and profound diversity in American thought. Although Santayana's thought is clearly original in both content and style, practically every important theme in his philosophy is shared in some measure (even though there is little agreement) with other notable American thinkers. Furthermore, if the American mind is perchance uniquely voluntaristic, moral, and religious while Santayana's thought was essentially contemplative, aesthetic, and poetic, it is no less true that the American spirit is also notoriously, if not deeply, generous towards those who are different and generally concerned that the dissenter shall be fairly heard before he is summarily damned. Indeed, there is a great deal of evidence that apart from Whitehead, with whom Santayana shared the dubious misfortune of having been born elsewhere than in the United States, he was the most sophisticated, the least credulous, and the most gifted, even though by no means the most consistent or profound, of the recent so-called American philosophers. He knew the history of philosophy more thoroughly perhaps than any of the others; and although his training and knowledge in the sciences were, as he admitted, inadequate, the breadth of his knowledge and his appreciation of artistic and religious traditions remain unparalleled in the history of American thought. If his philosophy is not tightly knit logically, or if his mind was essentially literary rather than scientific or metaphysical in its predilections, this was not because he lacked analytical skills and logical powers but rather because he was convinced that philosophy as such is much closer in method and aim to poetry and religion than to logic and science. To him philosophy was essentially a way of life, "a discipline of the mind and heart, a lay religion,"[6] rather than a mode of demonstrative argument or a special method of discovery and proof. Or as he said in a letter to William James in 1887, while he was still a student, he regarded philosophy as "an attempt to express a half-discovered reality, just as art is, and that two different renderings, if they are expressive, far from cancelling each other add to each other's value."[7] Yet his most sustained arguments are nonetheless paradigms of penetrating insight and logical coherence expressed in prose that fails to be lucid chiefly because of the richness of both its eloquence and its content.

Yet John E. Smith is by no means alone in calling Santayana's philosophic powers and credentials into question; it is not only the "American" character of his philosophy that is today challenged but also his very right to the title "philosopher." Many of the current practitioners of linguistic analysis, who suppose that philosophy is basically a method of clarifying or solving the puzzles and perplexities that arise out of the misuse of language, have little or no sympathy or respect for the view, no matter how ancient and perennial, that philosophy is primarily "a discipline of the mind and heart." Others hold the view, shared in important respects by Peirce and Dewey and to some extent even by James, that philosophy is basically an extension of scientific methods of inquiry, or "the 'laboratory habit of mind' extended into every area where inquiry may be fruitfully carried on."[8] Those who so conceive philosophy find it quite paradoxical to assert, as Santayana did, that "My philosophy neither is nor wishes to be scientific."[9] Nor can they regard the arts and poetry as seriously as he did. Of course both the analysts and those who insist that philosophy must be scientific would perhaps agree in a sense with his claim that "it would be a foolish philosophy that should ignore the continuities and analogies that run through the universe and that at once impress the attentive poet"[10]; they would, however, insist also that philosophers can and must deal with such continuities and analogies only analytically or scientifically, and not poetically. Contrary to Santayana's approach, much of contemporary philosophy is thus based on the premise that poetry and philosophy, though perhaps not altogether incompatible or mutually exclusive, have little if anything at all in common. Poetry may sometimes be the subject of philosophical interest and analysis; but the method, mood, and aim of philosophy, it is very widely assumed, can never be appropriately poetic or lyrical.

From other directions also the works of Santayana are

often regarded as essentially nonphilosophical. In certain important respects he may be favorably and fruitfully compared to the phenomenologists, who attempt a detailed description of experience on the assumption that every feature and quality of it—whether pain, anxiety, or joy—may be equally indicative of the actual character of existence. But Santayana was apparently never deeply troubled by the severe winds of anxiety and the terrible dread of nonbeing that have transformed so much of current phenomenology into ontological concern and existential analysis. Thus from the existential perspective he was not a genuine philosopher because he was preoccupied with essence rather than existence—or with eternal forms and with what he regarded as the *imaginative* and *aesthetic* landscapes envisioned or articulated by the religions and the arts. Consequently, according to the existentialists, he was unable to deal seriously or philosophically with the most important characteristics of existence—the concrete and problematic concerns—that are presumably both the source and the result of man's anguished but nonetheless accurate recognition of the basic irrationality or absurdity at the very heart of his condition.

Still others, perhaps less explicit in their charges but generally from the perspective of some traditional religious or metaphysical commitment, are convinced that because he began with first principles that are patently false or inadequate—with metaphysical materialism, atheism, or political and moral conservatism or relativism—Santayana cannot (or at least *ought* not to) be taken seriously as a philosopher.

Such negative views, it must be admitted, are not completely unjustified. Each at least identifies in its own way an important characteristic, though surely not in every case a characteristic fault, of Santayana's thought. Yet neither one nor all together succeed either in substantiating the charge that he does not deserve the title "philosopher" or in establishing the claim that he should not be taken seriously in the philosophical arena. In regard to the claim that he was essentially a poet and therefore not a philosopher, it should be quite sufficient simply to point out that historically philosophers have certainly been no less concerned with the poetic powers and qualities of experience and language than with the structural and logical forms of existence and discourse. Inspired mainly perhaps by the dialogues of Plato, philosophers have very often assumed, in practice if not also in theory, that there are indeed significant and apparently irreducible aspects of existence which can be conceived and articulated only in poetic terms—or in qualitative rather than logical categories. Even John Dewey, devoted as he was to the methods of science, emphasized, even more than he did the importance of structures and relations, that "a qualitative and qualifying situation is present as the background and control of every experience."[11] Indeed philosophy, if one means by this term the great body of literature commonly so-called, has rarely (except perhaps in the most recent examples) been less concerned with the qualities of experience than with concepts and arguments. In other words, the aspects of experience that can apparently be expressed only artistically or religiously have seemed no less important on the whole than logic or the elements of existence that are subject to measurement and the evidence of observation in verifying claims about them. Therefore, to note that Santayana took the arts seriously and regarded philosophy as a lay religion does not indicate that he was not a philosopher but only that he disagreed with perhaps the majority of contemporary philosophers about first principles and priorities. It is at least still conceivable, much current opinion to the contrary notwithstanding, that he was in fact philosophically correct in observing that "To be essentially poetical [is] a virtue and not a vice in the mind."[12]

In regard to the existentialist claim that Santayana was not a philosopher because in his preoccupation with essence he failed to deal with the concrete and perplexing problems of men, it must be admitted that he regarded logical possibilities and imaginative ideals as much more interesting and in certain respects more important than actualities. "Perfection," he wrote, "is better than truth."[13]

Therefore, he did not believe, as the existentialists apparently do, that the most important task for the philosopher is to recognize and articulate the perplexities and absurdities which constantly plague and frustrate man's practical enterprises as well as his attempt to understand himself and the world. He agreed certainly that the life of man is terribly difficult and in many respects absurd or irrational; but this only confirmed his conviction of the value of the "spiritual life"—and in his terms this meant a life "which looks not to another world but to the beauty and perfection that this world suggests, approaches, and misses."[14] The best life, he suggested with Socrates and Plato, is the life of the mind dispassionately concerned with perfection—even though perfection is possible only in the imagination. Thus anyone who claims to take existential problems more seriously than he did is very apt to be only estimating the situation and the priorities differently. He was himself convinced, as later chapters will indicate in some detail, that knowledge of the ultimately real—which he thought is matter—can in fact never be literal or complete; or in slightly different terms, he was thoroughly convinced that there is never a one-to-one correspondence between *what is* and *man's knowledge of what is,* or that the *things that exist* must be quite different in themselves from *that which appears* to either sense or intellect. He claimed that "our senses, no less than our poetry and myth, clothe in human images the manifold processes of matter,"[15] and that the sciences are ultimately no less symbolic than the arts and religions. He was therefore also convinced that basic issues are ignored or that fundamental questions are begged when one philosopher accuses another of ignoring the clear and important facts. "You may stop at what stage you will," he wrote, "according to your sense of what is real and important; for what one man calls higher another man calls unreal."[16] All that can be known, he concluded, is essence—the form or quality that appears to some sense or faculty—and each person must finally decide for himself which appearances have existential (as opposed to merely imaginary or mental) character and import. This, he believed, *is* the existential condition of man. He would then no doubt have agreed that if a person finds that his own experience is best described in terms of absurdity, anxiety, nausea, and despair, he may legitimately employ such concepts and attach the highest degree of importance to the realities that such experiences supposedly reveal and the activities they inspire and justify. But this, he would also insist, neither forbids nor invalidates the use of other terms that are generated by different experiences and reflect existence from a different point of view and in a quite different light.

And finally the view that Santayana's first principles are false or inadequate simply begs all the complex issues that are presumably in question wherever philosophical inquiry is taken seriously as an important or indispensable part of the perpetually unfinished task of passing appropriate judgment on the various features, elements, and activities of existence. A philosopher is essentially only a person with considerable concern and skill in articulating and defending the basic principles he holds in regard to the truth (what is) and the good (what ought to be). And until all the evidence is in and the philosophical task has been completed, which seems utterly improbable in the near or foreseeable future, disagreement with any system of thought so fully and finely articulated as Santayana's must be an equally defensible and serious exploration of the apparently basic features of existence and the qualities of experience which seem to be at once the most desirable and also attainable. It is clearly not sufficient simply to issue categorical denials of the premises of the view in question.

It may indeed be the case that Santayana's fundamental principles are all false—I myself can share none of them completely—but that many of his claims about particular matters of fact and importance are nonetheless highly relevant and revealing. Philosophies as well as the sciences, arts, and religions must evidently be judged not only by the apparent and enduring truth of their basic premises; they must be judged also by their fruitfulness in the ongoing enterprises through which men are presumably able to understand themselves and the universe, at least in some small measure, and to choose propitiously from among the many possibilities of good and evil.

Santayana was deeply concerned, like all serious-minded men, not to be deceived or to understand and judge existence in the terms and accents that are most nearly true and also fruitful. If the aim of philosophy may be said to be not simply conceptual truth or accurate logical models for interpreting every aspect of existence but equally the achievement of specifiable qualities of thought and life through appropriate choice and action, then Santayana was surely a philosopher. Even though his general theory of the nature of existence (or metaphysics) may be false, his account of the basis and nature of knowledge inconsistent or even in certain respects self-contradictory, and his moral theory simply an expression of his own preferences and prejudices, he nonetheless articulated with extraordinary concern and skill an elaborate view of man's existential character and environment. This view presumably renders certain values or modes of living ultimately more reasonable and desirable than others. And even though his system of thought may on the whole be more nearly false than true, it may nonetheless also help greatly to clarify our own vision of the truth we seek and the good we ought to do.

Chapter 2

LIFE AND CHARACTER

> "The spirit in me felt itself cast upon this social and political world somewhat like Robinson Crusoe upon his island."
>
> *My Host the World*

Jorge Agustin de Santayana—as he was christened in the parish church of San Marcos in Madrid on New Year's

Day, 1864—was born in that city on December 16, 1863. By a very unusual set of circumstances and events this "child born in Spain of Spanish parents" was "to be educated in Boston and to write in the English language."[1] The only child of the second marriage of his mother, Doña Josefina Borras, native of Glasgow, George Santayana was destined for Boston, and a largely unwanted career in philosophy at Harvard University, primarily by the fact that his mother had earlier been married to one George Sturgis of Boston. This marriage had occurred in 1849 in Manila, where his mother had already met Don Agustin Ruiz de Santayana, a native of Zamora, Spain, and a member of the Spanish civil service, who was to become her second husband in 1862, six years after the death of George Sturgis had left her a widow with three children. (For on a visit to Spain from Boston, where she had already established a household close to the Sturgis family, the widow Sturgis met again and married Don Agustin Ruiz de Santayana.)

When his mother returned to Boston in 1866 in order to bring up and educate her Sturgis children there, in accordance with a promise to their father, three-year-old George Santayana was left with his father in Ávila, the "ancient and noble town" where the "headquarters" of the Spanish side of the family was located. In 1872, however, Agustin Santayana brought his nine-year-old son to Boston, where the boy remained with his mother, brother, and two sisters when his father returned to Spain about a year later. His sister, Susana Sturgis, who was then twenty-one years old, began immediately to teach him to speak English. His progress was such that soon, according to his own report, he was able to speak "much better than Susana or . . . most of the boys in my successive schools."[2] A quiet and studious child, he "played no games, but sat at home all the afternoon and evening reading or drawing; especially devouring anything I could find that regarded religion, architecture, or geography."[3] According to a schoolmate, "The boys in Boston were wont to tease him in high school . . . but a sharp tongue and a fiery temper made him well able to take care of himself."[4] He was, he said himself, unhappy at home while school "was all dead routine, and insufficient" until he "formed close friendships and awoke to literature" during the last two or three years before college.[5]

By his own account certain important features of his mature philosophy, or at least sensitivities and attitudes that greatly influenced his later thought, were evident even during childhood and youth. Writing about a ride on the coachman's box of a carriage when he was seven, he suggested that his theory of essence, certainly a central element in the latest phases of his thought, was foreshadowed in the quality of his perceptions on that occasion. "From the coachman's box," he said, "my young mind saw nothing but the aesthetics of mechanism."[6] In other words, he identified forms and relations but not connections or causes. Perhaps characteristic of the same turn of mind and memory, as well as interesting in itself, is his account of "a sort of *amourette*" when he was ten. "I remember the child perfectly. She had a dark complexion and curly black hair, and stood very straight but gracefully. She was the first example to me of that admirable virtue cultivated by French actresses; eloquent stillness."[7] Not many years later, according to his report, he was also, in contrast to his sister, Susana, who "thought religion a matter of fact, like the geography of the Fiji Islands and the ways of the natives there," already "aware, at first instinctively and soon quite clearly on historical and psychological grounds, that religion and all philosophy of that kind was *invented*."[8] This claim was elaborated in one of his earliest works, *Interpretations of Poetry and Religion;* and he never abandoned the central thesis of the book: that religions are in large part only imaginative renderings of moral principles, or in terms he later used, that they "celebrate inevitable human passions and joyful hopes." That he did not regard this as an altogether critical indictment or indicative of the complete worthlessness of religion, however, is evident from the fact that he often visited the Cathedral at Ávila and "lingered there with the most pleasure," always "pleased and consoled" by this symbol that "Everything profound, everything beautiful had not yet vanished from the world."[10] His religious and aesthetic sensitivity and sympathies, as well as other elements of his intellectual temper, are apparent also in his account of the differences he noted between the Catholic Masses he attended very early and voluntarily on Sundays and the services later at the Unitarian church he "was being taken to against" his will. At the Masses, conducted for a German-speaking community, he said, "hymns were sung in unison, simply, gladly, and unaffectedly, yet rather musically." But in the Unitarian church he had to listen to "the perfunctory, inaudible pretense at keeping up with the paid quartet that was really performing" and to "a sermon like the leading article in some superior newspaper, calculated to confirm the conviction already in them that their bourgeois virtues were quite sufficient and that perhaps in time poor backward races and nations might be led to acquire them."[11]

Although the young Santayana learned English quickly and well, he confessed that he was "far" from the head of his class in school; but he added quickly, "I was not bad at my studies and got six honourable mentions in my Harvard entrance examinations."[12] He entered Harvard as a freshman in the fall of 1882. His first year apparently was intellectually uneventful. Although he failed a half-course in algebra, he did "well enough in the rest of the prescribed mathematics, analytic geometry," in which he "had had some grounding in school." His difficulty was due basically, he thought, to unimaginative teaching. "If my teachers had begun by telling me that mathematics was pure play with presuppositions, and wholly in the air, I might have become a good mathematician, because I am happy enough in the realm of essence. But they were overworked drudges, and I was largely inattentive, and inclined lazily to attribute to incapacity in myself or to a literary temperament that dullness which perhaps was due simply to lack of initiation."[13] The event of the college year that he remembered with most pleasure was that "towards the end of it" his mother announced that during the following summer he was to visit his father in Spain. This of course was to be only the first of many return visits to Europe before he finally went there in 1912 to remain for the rest of his life. But the news that he was to spend the summer of 1883 in this manner remained particularly memorable because it was his first opportunity to fulfill a longing "to travel, to see again with my own eyes old towns, cathedrals, castles, and palaces, and also the classic landscapes of Europe."[14] The trip was itself marred, however, at least slightly, by a "mild case" of smallpox and by a "plot" among aunts and uncles to marry him to a cousin whose "mind was common, and sometimes also her manners."[15]

Returning to Harvard after the visit to Spain, Santayana read for the first time the Roman poet, Lucretius; and the philosophic perspective and presuppositions of this poet were to remain in certain important respects a permanent model and inspiration. For he found in Lucretius poetic eloquence as well as an attitude and ideas that pleased him. "Even the physical and biological theories seemed instructive, not as scientific finalities, if science could be final, but as serving to dispel the notion that anything is non-natural or miraculous." Lucretius had insisted that there are purely natural or materialistic and mechanical causes of all the various phenomena of existence. This view appealed to the college sophomore and eventually became one of his "first principles." In his own terms the principle was, "not that a particular philosophy called naturalism must be true *a priori,* but that nature sets the standards of naturalness."[16]

From childhood to old age Santayana often expressed his feelings and thoughts in poetic form. He wrote his first sonnet in 1884. This poem, he said later, reflected what he had first felt at sixteen rather than at twenty. "But I still recognized," he added, "as I recognize now at nearly eighty, the legitimacy of that feeling."[17] Thus the poem is worth quoting partly because it articulated, though the author was only twenty, attitudes and ideas that were to remain integral elements in the thought of the mature man and philosopher:

O world, thou choosest not the better part!
It is not wisdom to be only wise,
And on the inward vision close the eyes,
But it is wisdom to believe the heart.
Columbus found a world, and had no chart,
Save one that faith deciphered in the skies;
To trust the soul's invincible surmise
Was all his science and his only art.
Our knowledge is a torch of smoky pine
That lights the pathway but one step ahead
Across a void of mystery and dread.
Bid, then, the tender light of faith to shine
By which the mortal heart is led
Unto the thinking of the thought divine.[18]

Of course, for the older philosopher, as will become clear later, "the heart" that wisdom must trust was by no means divine revelation or inspiration, as the poem clearly meant originally, but natural impulses and the reason or order that may be evident as a harmony among different desires and needs; and eventually "dread," if not also "mystery," was largely dissolved in philosophic materialism and "Epicurean contentment in being an accident in an accident."[19] "Faith" became "animal faith" or instinctive belief in the reliability of impulse and perception; "the thinking of the thought divine" came to mean essentially the imaginative perfection of a world that seemed actually and terribly imperfect. Only the symbol of knowledge, as "a torch of smoky pine/ That lights the pathway but one step ahead," remained radically appropriate in the later thought of the philosopher who insisted that science as well as common sense is often "uncritically based on animal faith and empirical presumption." Yet, if "the heart" may also be regarded as an instinctive affection for the spontaneous and imaginative vistas of the arts and religions, and "knowledge" as primarily the recognition of "facts" that are, in Santayana's words, "at once ugly, obscure, and unsubstantial,"[20] then this first early sonnet is surprisingly prophetic of the direction of his later thought.

In 1886, having graduated from Harvard *summa cum laude,* Santayana shared the Walker Fellowship, "usually awarded to graduates who wished to study philosophy in Germany,"[21] with a classmate, C. A. Strong. In Germany, however, except for a moderate enthusiasm for the works of Arthur Schopenhauer, he found little to his liking in either thought or culture. But he blamed only himself. "I was too much enveloped in my American (and afterwards in my English) associations to lose myself in the German scene, to learn German properly, and to turn a copious German 'spiritual' stream into my private channel." Apart from attending lectures, he lived largely alone. "There were no people with whom I cared to talk; and my punishment was that I never learned to speak the language."[22] He nonetheless listened with great personal and intellectual interest to Professor Friedrich Paulsen on the Greeks and Spinoza, and "was thus settled" in the naturalist convictions that had begun with his reading of Lucretius. In the Greeks and Spinoza, he said, he found "revealed the real background, the true and safe foundation, for human courage, human reason, and human imagination." They combined, he thought, in "spontaneous agreement," "the two insights that for me were essential: naturalism as to the origin and history of mankind, and fidelity, in moral sentiment, to the inspiration of reason, by which the human mind conceives truth and eternity and participates in them ideally."[23] But though he acknowledged a clear gain philosophically, he confessed that he "was wholly incapable of taking a Doctor's degree in Germany."[24] At the end of the first semester in fact he went to England for a visit and remained at Oxford for the rest of the year, finding "England infinitely more interesting and stimulating than Germany."[25] He did, however, return dutifully to Berlin the next year when, after Strong had given up his share in the Walker Fellowship, it was awarded to him alone.

Santayana returned to America in 1888 and suggested to Josiah Royce that he should write his thesis for the doctorate on the philosophy of Schopenhauer. But Royce, not impressed by or sympathetic to Schopenhauer's pessimistic views, proposed instead a study of the *Microcosmos* of Rudolf Hermann Lotze (1817–1881). This thesis for the doctorate, entitled *Lotze's System of Philosophy,* was duly completed during the academic year. It was not a distinguished thesis but clearly a competent one that contained impressive evidence of critical skills and philosophic understanding. Consequently in the fall of 1889 Santayana was invited to join the department of philosophy primarily to teach a single course on Locke, Berkeley, and Hume, from which William James wished to be relieved. Immediately after the beginning of the term, however, a second course, on Descartes, Spinoza, and Leibniz, was added when the professor who regularly offered the course resigned. Thus began a teaching career in philosophy at Harvard that was to continue for more than twenty-two years, though he said later about his life and career in America that "if I had been free to choose, I should not have lived there, or been educated there, or taught philosophy there or anywhere else."[26] Yet his first philosophical work, *The Sense of Beauty,* was admittedly the direct result a few years later of his preparation for a course in aesthetics. And although it may be true, as he said in his old age, that the argument of this first book was "uninspired and academic,"[27] it was also without precedent and for a long time the most influential work on the subject in America. It also made his academic position at Harvard more secure. Less than ten years later the five volumes of *The Life of Reason* appeared; the ground work for this too had been laid by a course which he offered for several years entitled, "The Philosophy of History," though the work was also influenced by "systematic reading of Plato and Aristotle" during a year's leave of absence which he spent at Trinity College, Cambridge.[28] Obviously he must have approached his work as a teacher of philosophy with considerable enthusiasm as well as energy and intelligence.

Meanwhile the direction and temper of his philosophical reflections had been largely determined by what he came to regard as the "moral settlement" that occurred primarily as a result of the combined circumstances and events of his thirtieth year. According to his own report, although there was no revolution, conversion, or radical change of heart, "four thoughts" merged their currents during this year and carried him "irresistibly towards the same sea: youth was past, friendship had had its day, the future offered me nothing that I cared for, religion and social utopias proposed nothing that I respected."[29] Each of these "thoughts" was closely and significantly related to either special circumstances or a specific event. First of all, at least in retrospect, he identified the age of thirty itself, for "a poet and a lover of youth," as grounds enough for transformation or transition. For instead of being now, as he had been for some years, a friend who shared the activities and pleasures of students, he had become merely "one of their masters." He was himself no longer young or the friend of the young. "That chapter had come to an end: yet youth, in the world's and in the poet's eyes, is perpetual. The platonic transition was therefore at once spontaneous and inevitable, from the many to the one, from the existent but transitory to the ideal and eternal."[30]

The specific events were, however, probably more important than mere age and circumstance. The "thought" that "friendship had had its day" found at least its symbol, if not also its cause, in the tragic death of a close friend, Warwick Potter, who was seven years younger than Santayana. "I didn't know how much attached to him I was," he wrote later, "until I heard the unexpected news that he had died. . . ."[31] He felt that he had lost his "last real friend" and eventually mourned the event in a series of four sonnets. There was the sense of irreparable loss:

With you a part of me has passed away;
For in the peopled forest of my mind
A tree made leafless by this wintery wind
Shall never don again its green array

. . . .

And I scarce know which part may greater be,—
What I keep of you, or you rob from me.[32]

There was the inevitable question *why:*

And I half know why heaven deemed it right
Your youth, and this my joy in youth should fail."[33]

But apparently there was also some mild comfort at least in the recognition that life poses dangers that even death does not know:

For time a sadder mask than death may spread
Over the face that ever should be young.[34]

But it was not simply Warwick's death, he wrote later, that inspired these sad lines. "It was the thought of everything that was escaping me: the Good in all the modes of it that I might have caught a glimpse of and lost."[35]

But even more poignantly symbolic to him of life and his own future was the death that same year of his father. His reaction to this event was complex and the final outcome was not so much a sense of loss but of apprehension. "I had never before seen anyone die, and that in itself is an impressive and sobering experience." It was this experience that was associated with the "thought" that "the future offered me nothing that I cared for." His father "was seventy-nine years old, deaf, half-blind, and poor." "The fact that he was my father . . . called up a lurid image of what my life in the world was likely to be; solitary, obscure, trivial, and wasted. I must not look ahead. Ahead, after youth was gone, everything would grow sadder and sadder. I must look within or above . . . into eternity."[36]

Perhaps most surprising, at least on the surface, is the fact that it was the marriage of his sister, Susana, that was the occasion for the "thought" that "religion and social utopias proposed nothing that I respected." Susana, his godmother at his christening and "really my spiritual mother," not only taught him English when he first came to America but taught him his prayers in English and his advanced catechism, and also initiated him "into theology, architecture, and polite society." She was, he said, perhaps "the greatest power, and certainly the strongest affection" in his life.[37] Although she was twelve years older than he, they shared the spiritual separation from their mother that occurred as they developed new interests, particularly their common interest in religion and the Church. Their interest in religion continued to grow in spite of their "mother's intense hostility to the Church."[38] But Susana had also to bear the blame, at least in the eyes of their mother, for the fact that the young George loved "images and church functions and the mysteries of theology" which she regarded as "dangerous and morbid."[39] Yet, as already suggested, Santayana and his sister approached religion from radically different points of view. He had recognized clearly by the time he was seventeen, he said, that religion is "poetry intervening in life," and suggested that this view "had really been native to me and congenital."[40] But Susana "became fanatical against her natural good sense, and worried about the salvation of her friends and relations as if that were not in God's hands, and as if the salvation of souls were a physical event, like the saving or drowning of passengers in a shipwreck."[41] Yet Santayana had admired her courage when she entered for a time during his college days a convent in Baltimore "in showing such contempt of the world." But her marriage at the age of forty-one to a Catholic widower with six children only displeased and disheartened him, in part because it seemed "an act of desperation on her part, a redoubled proof of her weakness." But the event became also "in some measure a disillusionment about Catholicism" because her marriage seemed so clearly a result of "craving for moral support and social backing in religion and in her self-esteem."[42] He thought her marriage merely continued her fight "against all dramatic insight or transcendental laughter" in respect to religion.[43] He concluded therefore that in effect her religion only burdened her life with superstition and otherworldliness, instead of providing, as religion should, "inward liberation and peace."[44]

So in his thirtieth year Santayana found himself a teacher of philosophy at Harvard—where philosophy was "most modern, most deeply Protestant, most hopefully new," all of which he disliked intensely—and also disillusioned about most of the things he had come to love or care for. He expected the future to become "sadder and sadder." If he had been more lyrical, he might have said with Dylan Thomas:

> And the true
> Joy of the long-dead child sang burning
> In the sun.
> It was my thirtieth
> Year to heaven stood there in the summer noon
> Though the town below lay leaved with October
>   blood.[45]

What he did say was that he had "made progress on the primrose path of Epicurean wisdom."[46] Externally, however, his life did not change. "I went on teaching and writing, drinking and travelling and making friends; only that now and beforehand and explicitly, these occupations were marked for me with a cross: the sign on the one hand of death and on the other of consecration." The change had been "gradual and bloodless" but not without "a wrench," "a passage through dark night" that led however "quickly back into the light, into the pure starlight that transports without dazzling." His own intellectual and spiritual interests remained essentially the same; but his attitude towards them and his expectations were radically changed. He said to himself now: "Cultivate imagination, love it, give it endless forms, but do not let it deceive you. Enjoy the world, travel over it, and learn its ways, but do not let it hold you. . . . To possess things and persons in idea is the only pure good to be got out of them; to possess them physically or legally is a burden and a snare."[47] Subsequently he composed a second sequence of sonnets in which the key line, he said, was,

A perfect love is founded on despair.[48] (In the edition of 1921 the line reads, *A perfect love is nourished by despair.)* Yet the series ends with a poetic affirmation:

> Though utter death should swallow up my hope
> And choke with dust the mouth of my desire,
> Though no dawn burst, and no aurorean choir
> Sing *Gloria Deo* when the heavens ope,
> Yet I have light of love, nor need to grope
> Lost, wholly lost, without an inward fire;
> The flame that quickeneth the world entire
> Leaps in my breast, with cruel death to cope.
>
> . . . .
>
> One love sufficeth an eternity.[49]

Two years later, in 1896, this approach to life was presumably given important philosophical support by his studies during his sabbatical year at Cambridge University. The year was spent in reading Plato and Aristotle with "Henry Jackson as Tutor, and with Bertie Russell, G. E. Moore, and MacTaggart as philosophical friends."[50] Apparently the most influential aspect of the year's experience for Santayana was Jackson's analysis of the concept of Being contained in Plato's *Parmenides.* Not only did this analysis help him to understand Plato, he claimed, but also enabled him "to see that Being, the One, the Many, *et cetra* [*sic*], were names of categories, not of existent things, so that all cosmological theories relying on dialectic (such as that of Leibniz) were sophistical. They played with essences and thought they were disclosing facts."[51] The stage was now completely set for the development of the "philosophy of ultimate disillusion." The rest of his long life was to be primarily extensive, careful, and eloquent reflection on the scepticism, resignation, and disillusion which he thought must accompany any love or claim that was to be clear and completely unmistaken about the character of its object, and thus wholly free of unrealistic assumptions and expectations.

In his maturity Santayana was, at least to many, an attractive person and a "greatly admired teacher."[52] Perhaps the best verbal portrait is by Margaret Munsterberg, the daughter of one of his colleagues, who saw him frequently:

> In his dark Spanish eyes there was a sudden illumination, an extraordinary focusing of light rays having the effect of a blaze of pure spirit. His face was handsome, delicate, pale against the black hair and small mustache; it seemed the face of a dreamer rather than of a scholarly thinker. But his eyes had sprites in them and a light from fairy-lands forlorn. . . . And then his laugh! He laughed . . . with his whole face. His was a laugh to delight a child's heart, the laugh of Peter Pan, brimming over with pure merriment.[53]

Baker Brownell, one of his students during his last years at Harvard, remembered him as "a dark, gentle looking man, unobtrusive, medium sized."

> He was quietly dressed, neither arty nor academic, and usually wore fastidious, faintly trans-Atlantic black. Within his quietness one discerned a distinguished manner, grace, reticent pride; and he had beautiful eyes. He was bald, rather tragically so, we students thought, but he had a handsome and philosophic beard that later gave way to more handsome though less philosophic mustaches without a beard. His lectures were quiet, gently spoken. . . . Usually he sat in his chair, his musing hands before him, gave his lecture or carried on a leisurely class discussion, and when the bell rang, stopped.[54]

Two aspects of Santayana's character and intellect demand further notice. The first of these is his *wit.* Surely few philosophers have ever been his equal in turning the truly clever and striking phrase. Sometimes the phrase was sardonic, a piercing jab at an associate, critic, or idea. But equally often it was simply the delightful leap or caper of a mind thoroughly at home with its subject matter and instruments. A few examples must suffice to illustrate this quality. Perhaps one of the more impish and unexpected examples occurs in a discussion of "liberalism and love." "British liberalism," he wrote, "has been particularly cruel to love; in the Victorian era all its amiable impulses were reputed indecent, until a marriage certificate suddenly rendered them godly, though still unmentionable."[55] More typical, however, is his suggestion that to claim that one thing is better than another intrinsically or without any relation to other things is like insisting that "whiskey is more intoxicating in itself, without reference to any animal; that it is pervaded as it were, by an inherent intoxication, and stands dead drunk in its bottle."[56] And he characterized the idealistic doctrine that harmony and agreement are the criteria of truth as simply another form of the argument that "We go right enough, darling, if we go wrong together."[57]

More obvious and celebrated than his wit—though not more important or more characteristic of the man—was his so-called *detachment.* His sister, Susana, commented on the fact that he was detached even as a youth.[58] Also his own descriptions of himself bear witness to, and in some measure account for, an unusual degree of detachment. As a young man, he said, he felt divided from his contemporaries at Harvard by "initial divergencies of race, country, religion, and career."[59] But the matter clearly went much deeper than such largely superficial differences. "Not only my body," he observed, "but my rather special and difficult relations to persons and places seemed clearly imposed facts; and . . . my personal tastes and feelings became early apparent, and caused me to feel that I lived in a kind of solitude, not transcendental and spiritual, but decidedly solitariness in a crowd and foreignness among very distinct people."[60] He "liked solitude in crowds, meals in restaurants, walks in public parks, architectural rambles in noble cities" and "wished to remain a visitor, looking in at the cages."[61] He compared himself to a "small utterly insecure waif" and to

"Robinson Crusoe upon his island." "And as the feeling of being a stranger and an exile by nature grew upon me in time, it came to be almost a point of pride."[62] In the eyes of certain critics this detachment appeared to be aristocratic snobbishness; to others it appeared as callous indifference to the suffering and need of mankind or as an inordinate preoccupation with beauty and perfection. To still others it seemed "compassionate understanding" and "neither indifference nor propaganda" but "both simply and profoundly, philosophy" or "a candid wisdom, classically bred."[63] According to Santayana himself, "Detachment leaves you content to be where you are, and what you are. Why should you hanker to be elsewhere or someone else? Yet in your physical particularity detachment makes you ideally impartial; and in enlightening your mind it is likely to render your action also more successful and generous."[64] Indeed mind (or *spirit,* as he preferred to call it) is, he thought, by its very nature detached and contemplative, a witness and not an actor in the flux of existence.

The desire to make his detachment as complete as possible, to be free to think and write without institutional or professional obligations or impediments, led Santayana, when he was only fifty, to leave Harvard and teaching forever. Indeed as early as 1888, when he was barely twenty-five, he had begun deliberately to prepare for a life of leisure later. "I began that year to save, and to possess a little capital. In other words, I began to prepare for my retirement from teaching before I had begun to teach."[65] His career at Harvard had, in his own eyes, been long as well as "slow and insecure, made in an atmosphere of mingled favour and distrust."[66] His colleagues in philosophy had supported him; he had the "goodwill and kindness" of William James. He said of James, however, "I trusted his heart but I didn't respect his judgment" and that James "would have liked me less if he had understood me better."[67] On the whole, he was convinced, he had been "disliked" but "swallowed." Thus when his mother died in 1911, leaving him a legacy that would now be supplemented by earnings from his own writings as well as by savings, he promptly decided to begin at once living as he had always wanted to live. In January 1912 he resigned his professorship at Harvard and went immediately to Europe. His "official career had happily come to an end."[68] He never returned again to Boston or to America.

Santayana spent the war years of 1914–1918 in England. In addition to lectures, some given earlier in France and some in England, and published as *Character and Opinion in the United States,* he completed two other books during these years; these were *Egotism in German Philosophy* and *Soliloquies in England.* These three books together, he said, marked his "emancipation from official control and professional pretensions."[69] *Soliloquies in England* in particular, apart from its great intrinsic interest, is profoundly important for its introduction of the themes and attitudes that were to characterize most of his later work. In his own words, "There was no occasion to change my subjects, to abandon even technical philosophy or my interest in academic life and the humanities. But all was now a voluntary study, a satirical survey, a free reconsideration: the point of view had become at once frankly personal and speculatively transcendental. A spirit, the spirit in a stray individual, was settling its accounts with the universe."[70] He loved England very much and was tempted to remain there permanently; but he perceived, he said, that he was "in danger of losing my philosophic cruelty and independence."[71] Also, at least in retrospect, he *felt* "the tyrant flood of democracy in England and of commercial imperialism in America, visibly undermining my England in England and swallowing up my America in America. I was protecting, by fleeing from both, the memory of them in myself."[72]

Soon after the war Santayana returned to the Continent, chiefly to Rome, although he continued to visit Susana in Ávila, sometimes for an entire summer, until her death in 1928. But the remainder of his life was largely a life of reflection, and an account of it must be primarily a critical examination of the ideas he cherished and elaborated. In an essay left unpublished at his death, he wrote, "I can identify myself heartily with nothing in me except with the flame of spirit itself. Therefore the truest picture of my inmost being would show none of the features of my person, and nothing of the background of my life. It would show only the light of the understanding that burned within me and, as far as it could, consumed and purified all the rest."[73] Insofar as this is true at all, it is especially true of his later years. Yet it should be noted here that his most popular book, a novel, was not published until 1936. *The Last Puritan: A Memoir in the Form of a Novel* was a book club selection and not only made his old age financially more secure but also greatly increased the scope of his reputation as a man of letters. His final book, *Dominations and Powers,* was surely influenced—though one could by no means say *inspired*—by the war of 1939–1945; for, as he said, he "lived through it in Rome in monastic retirement, with the visible and audible rush of bombing aeroplanes over my head, and of invading armies before my eyes."[74] This fact only intensified the disillusion, the sense of the ultimate helplessness of the individual, and the conviction that the only wisdom is in detachment and resignation—all of which, as will become clear, are central elements of his thought. "The contemporary world," he said, "has turned its back on the attempt and even on the desire to live reasonably. The two great wars (so far) of the twentieth century were adventures in enthusiastic unreason."[75] Yet he wrote in a letter to a friend, "The Old World is impoverished, but still beautiful."[76]

Santayana spent his final years in the Calvary Hospital in Rome where he was cared for by the Sisters of the Little Company of Mary, commonly called the "Blue Sisters." He died there on September 26, 1952, hardly three months short of his eighty-ninth birthday, and was buried in the Catholic cemetery in the space provided for Spanish citizens. In *The Poet's Testament,* which had not been published but was read at his funeral, he observed, apparently with gratitude, that he had been "Spared by the Furies," that "the Fates were kind," and that neither "fear, nor hope, nor envy saw my face." Just how true these words were there is of course no way to know except by consulting his work. There one does indeed find an equanimity perhaps possible, particularly to a sensitive man, only in the absence of fear and hope and envy. But in the same poem he also expressed, in perhaps his most lyrical lines, a more positive and central element of his thought:

> To trembling harmonies of field and cloud,
> Of flesh and spirit, was my worship vowed.
> Let form, let music, let the all-quickening air
> Fulfill in beauty my imperfect prayer.[77]

Chapter 3

MATTER AND SPIRIT

> "I know but this, that daily as I plod
> Amid the ruined labours of mankind,
> I shed the flesh awhile, becoming mind."
>
> "Spirit," *The Poet's Testament*

No conjunction of terms is more indicative of George Santayana's unique philosophical perspective, of the chief themes and the paradoxes of his thought, than "matter and spirit." He often thought of himself as the only consistent defender of philosophic materialism among contemporary thinkers and sometimes even as the only philosopher who really understood that the value of the spiritual life is due to its intrinsic character and not to its origin or supposed consequences. He attempted in any case to combine a thoroughgoing materialism with a genuine appreciation of "spiritual values" as they appear in the arts and religions, in knowledge and contemplation. Apparently this unorthodox combination of fundamental categories was not designed primarily to influence the thought of other philosophers but only to justify a particular way of life—a way that might, he thought, perchance be emulated by a few kindred spirits. But basic philosophical problems are not of course mitigated by modest aims, and one important task in understanding and evaluating Santayana's philosophy is to look carefully at his attempt to understand consciousness (or *spirit)* and intellectual (or spiritual) values in terms of a system that is basically materialistic.

The problem of the origin and nature of consciousness is indeed the nemesis not only of the materialist but of anyone who supposes that philosophic inquiry can begin as most other inquiries begin—on the assumption that the problems, if they are genuine, can be neatly formulated and definitely solved. The *existence* of *consciousness,* if the words may be understood for the moment in prephilosophical innocence, is apparently the necessary condition of recognizing problems of any kind. Yet the question of whether or not *consciousness* should be said to *exist* has plagued philosophy even from its very beginnings; and recent American philosophy in particular is filled with ambiguities and enormous difficulties as the results of its attempts to reach a satisfactory view of the place and character of consciousness in the order of being.

Now a great deal of reflective analysis or philosophical sophistication is by no means required to see that existence may be readily, if not altogether accurately, divided into two radically different parts: the *experienced* and the *experiencer,* the *perceived* and the *perceiver,* the *known* and the *knower.* It is obviously not easy, however, if it is possible at all, to say what either of these is when considered independently. Consequently in much philosophical inquiry there has been a tendency when common sense dualism—or the view that mind and matter are equally real and independent—has come into question to reduce the one to the other, that is, either to try to understand the object known as simply the idea or creation of the knower, *or* to comprehend consciousness as somehow a product of material organization and process. Such views have generally, though not necessarily, occurred as reactions to dualism or out of dissatisfaction with the claim that consciousness and the objects of consciousness, or mind and body, are two completely different substances bound together temporarily but by no means functionally or actually inseparable.

Santayana's views of consciousness developed in an age and context in which each of these three ways of regarding mind and body was viable and defended by one or more important thinker. The traditional dualism of Christianity, as developed by St. Augustine and Descartes especially, was of course represented by many. One eloquent opponent of such dualism was the idealist, Josiah Royce, who was an effective spokesman at Harvard for the claim that the *object of thought* is "nothing whatever but the idea's own conscious purpose or will" and that "the world of my idea is simply my own will itself determinately embodied."[1] At the opposite extreme were a number of thinkers influenced by the immense progress in physics and by the theory of evolution—for example, Chauncey Wright, T. H. Huxley, and later but prior to Santayana's own major statements on the topic, John B. Watson—who were convinced that consciousness and the sequences of thought are ultimately only the results of physical and chemical changes occurring automatically in the nervous system. The further implication of this claim, as some recognized, was of course that thinking or thought is essentially an effect—and never a cause—which occurs when material organization and processes happen to be favorable. This was the view that Santayana, with his own characteristic emphases and modifications, defended from the very beginning of his independent philosophical career. The virtues and faults of the doctrine can perhaps be best understood over against trends and claims that were in fundamental disagreement with such complete materialism.

But first a few words should be said about Santayana's use of a terminology that is basically different from the terminology of most other contemporary philosophers who have dealt with this problem. First of all, he distinguished sharply between the *psyche* (soul) and *spirit* (mind). The first he described as the hereditary and automatic order of life—the principle of growth, instinct, impulse, and action. Every organism or living creature is therefore besouled or possesses a psyche. Spirit, however, arises only when the life of the psyche is complex and stable enough to produce and sustain not only impulses, desires, and actions but also the simultaneous awareness of these. Also, as already suggested, he used the word "spirit" where others have generally used "mind" or "consciousness." His own explanation was that "In modern philosophy the notion of mind has become confused and treacherous, so that in whatever direction we press it into consistency, mind ceases to be mind."[2] He thought that in particular there was inevitable obfuscation in the tendency to assimilate the concept of mind (or spirit) to such related notions as the ego, behavior, feeling, or the whole of life and will, or the effort to derive it from an unconscious but feeling substance that presumably gives rise to both "organic bodies and centres of apprehension." The "living mind," he insisted, "is none of those things."[3]

No doubt his choice of terms was influenced in some measure by William James's denial that consciousness exists, or by what might perhaps be better described as James's attempt to conceive consciousness without departing from the principle of parsimony that is the ideal of science, and yet not to be reductive in the sense of expecting to derive mind from something so utterly different that the result is not simply mystery but absurdity. James's view was almost certainly among the accounts of mind that Santayana regarded as "confused and treacherous." And indeed James's treatment of consciousness was far from clear. But so were the views of the physicists and biologists with whom Santayana basically agreed in trying to give a materialistic account of the origins of mind.

It is also worth noting that the word "spirit" has poetic and religious connotations which are largely absent when one speaks of "mind" or "consciousness." And though Santayana was intellectually on the side of the scientists, temperamentally and morally he was clearly in the tradition of St. Augustine and Shelley. In any case he used the word "spirit" to denote the total awareness that distinguishes being awake from being asleep or as a near synonym for what others have generally called "mind" or "consciousness."

The major intellectual feature of the late nineteenth and early twentieth centuries with which the philosopher had to reckon was no doubt the theory of evolution. The speculation and research of Charles Darwin, published under the title *On the Origin of Species* in 1859, put into serious question, at least for the scientifically educated, the long accepted premise that man's way of being in the world is exceptional or unique; this included an effective challenge to the widespread and traditional assumption that mind is at least functionally, if not actually, separable from the body. Although materialists such as Democritus and Lucretius among the ancients as well as an increasing number of important modern thinkers had already found monistic implications in physics and biology, the theory of evolution was a more serious and dramatic challenge than anything in the past to both the idealistic and dualistic accounts of mind. Yet the implications of evolution for the nature of mind were by no means clear and unambiguous. On the one hand the theory, insofar as it suggested an automatic and mechanical process, seemed to support the epiphenomenalism of the materialists. This view claimed that mind is simply a concomitant—like the rainbow—of certain physical conditions and processes. In itself it is nothing and so causes nothing. But to such men as William James and Charles Sanders Peirce the theory of evolution, by providing at least the semblance of goal-seeking or purposive behavior, suggested that consciousness could by no means be adequately conceived as simply a useless appendage or an accidental emergent in the evolutionary development of nonliving and nonthinking substance. Mind must somehow be understood as an integral and indispensable element of the whole, or as a genuine cause and not only an effect in the evolutionary process. Consciousness or thought must be a function within—and not a wholly transcendent witness of—nature; it must be a participant in and not only a spectator of cosmic events, orders, and processes.

Peirce approached the problem by suggesting that what is ordinarily called matter is itself a form of "effete mind" —mind that is bound by "inveterate habits" or inertia. Materialism is completely unacceptable, he said, because "it requires us to suppose that a certain kind of mechanism will feel. . . ." Cartesian dualism, he claimed, is now quite simply indefensible, and neutralism (or the hypothesis that both mind and matter are derived ultimately from a single substance) violates the "logical maxim known as Ockham's razor, i.e., that not more independent elements are to be supposed than necessary."[4] The simplest explanation, in other words, must be considered truest. Thus Peirce defended a form of panpsychism or metaphysical idealism which did not deny the independent reality of the object of knowledge but did insist that consciousness is a fundamental and nonderivative feature of existence.

William James's approach to the issue was both more radical and more interesting, though not obviously or necessarily more reliable. So far as the form of his language is concerned, he literally denied the very existence of consciousness—that is, he denied that consciousness exists as an entity. The chief fact of experience to which he obviously wished to direct attention, however, was that consciousness is not itself a separate or observable element of the objective world. Consciousness is never an object. Instead, when we look for consciousness, James pointed out, what we find is this or that object: roundness, blueness, roughness, hotness, etc. The significant point is simply that there is no distinguishable *stuff* which can be identified as consciousness in the absence of or apart from objects. James himself in fact summed up his view by insisting that "Consciousness connotes a kind of external relation, and does not denote a special stuff or way of being."[5] This denial of the existence of consciousness was an integral and striking part of James's "radical empiricism," or the doctrine that experience is all that is ever known and that it is misleading to suppose that the distinction between *experience* and the *experienced,* or the *knower* and the *object,* is ever sharp or wholly reliable.

The claim that consciousness is a relation or a function rather than an entity became even more explicit and influential in the philosophy of John Dewey. "Ability to anticipate future consequences and to respond to them as stimuli to present behavior," Dewey wrote, "may well *define* what is meant by a mind or by consciousness."[6] Or in terms that will perhaps prove a better parallel to Santayana's views, Dewey claimed, "As life is a character of events in a peculiar condition of organization, and 'feeling' is a quality of life-forms marked by complexly mobile and discriminating responses, so 'mind' is an added property assumed by a feeling creature, when it reaches that organized interaction with other living creatures which is language, communication."[7] Yet Dewey was perfectly willing to admit that he found it impossible *to state* just what it means to be conscious, but "not because there is some mystery in or behind it, but for the same reason that we cannot tell just what sweet or red immediately is: it is something had, not communicated and known."[8] But he clearly preferred a concept of body-mind as a unified whole to the notion that two different kinds of entities exist and influence each other.

In at least one sense of the terms, then, it may be said that both James and Dewey denied the *existence* of *mind* or *consciousness.* But both, it is also clear, wished primarily to emphasize only that consciousness is not an element of existence such that its character and fortunes may be radically separable and different from the character and fortunes of the body and its environment. Santayana was convinced, however, that their language, if not their meaning, was profoundly in error. There can be little doubt that he was thinking of James and Dewey, among others, when he wrote that since spirit or mind is at least a "messenger of oncoming things," of dangers and opportunities, the suggestion, especially by a philosopher, that spirit or consciousness does not exist "may accordingly pass for a delicious absurdity, and the best of unconscious comedy." Indeed, he continued, "such a denial seems not only stupid, but ungracious; for a man ought to be proud of this dubious spark in his embers, and nurse it more tenderly than the life of a frail child." He admitted, however, that though the "language is rash and barbarous," those who deny the existence of spirit or consciousness "are honestly facing the facts and are on the trail of a truth."[9] That truth is, according to Santayana, that mind is not in any sense or measure a power or cause of anything at all. Mind exists but it is impotent. This thesis, always a major premise of his thought, was perhaps expressed most clearly and eloquently in his reflections at the commemoration of the tercentenary of the birth of Spinoza. So far as our knowledge and will are concerned, he said there, "existence is a miracle, and, morally considered, a free gift from moment to moment." And to make the point unmistakable, he added:

> Evidently all interconnections and sequence of events, and in particular any consequences which we may expect to flow from our actions, are really entirely beyond our spiritual control. When our will commands and seems, we know not how, to be obeyed by our bodies and by the world, we are like Joshua seeing the sun stand still at his bidding; when we command and nothing happens, we are like King Canute surprised that the rising tide should not obey him; and when we say we have executed a great work and re-directed the course of history, we are like Chanticleer attributing the sunrise to his crowing.

In other words, when the human spirit examines its own conditions frankly and candidly, he thought, the conclusion is inescapable that "though it is living, it is powerless to live; that though it may die, it is powerless to die; and that altogether, at every instant and in every particular, it is in the hands of some alien and inscrutable power."[10] His sense of utter dependence and his natural piety were clearly such that in a different age he might well have agreed with St. Augustine that the power by which one lives and thinks is the Holy, Truth, or God. Yet there is very little evidence—though his sense of both beauty and tragedy was in certain respects deep and extraordinary—that he ever actually experienced existence as Holy, or even as an "awful and wonderful excellence." In any case the denial of the existence of consciousness or spirit, he suggested, is at best an indirect and ill-conceived acknowledgment of the truth that all efficacy is in matter and that all events, including the events of the conscious or spiritual life, occur as they do only because of material processes or in spite of man's will and effort rather than because of them.

This was of course the very opposite of the "truth" that James and Dewey supposed they were articulating. For neither wished to deny in the least that consciousness, as an analytically distinguishable part of experience or body-mind, is indeed significantly responsible for the success or failure of the projects and processes in which it participates. And on this particular point they were evidently much closer to both common sense and the careful philosophic reflection that concludes, contrary to Santayana, that mind—as represented by the individual person who reflects upon and anticipates the course of events—can in nowise disclaim all responsibility for itself and its action. Freedom as well as dependence, it seems clear, must be attributed to man in nature. The fact that Chanticleer's crowing does not cause the sun to rise certainly does not imply the complete futility of all human purpose or the vanity of all effort and confidence.

Yet surely this disclaimer does not imply at all that Santayana's view of mind or spirit is in every respect mistaken or inferior to that of the pragmatists. Indeed he seems thoroughly justified in recognizing that there is not in fact the clear and neat unity between the knower and the known or mind and body that James and Dewey so much desired and sought. Instead the English philosopher, G. E. Moore, was perhaps closer to the immediate evidence of experience when he insisted that two distinct elements are involved in all reflective experience, "one which I call consciousness, and another which I call the object of consciousness." Briefly, Moore's analysis suggested that "blue is one object of sensation and green is another, and consciousness, which both sensations have in common, is different from either."[11] Santayana's account, insofar as it concerned the *phenomena* of consciousness as distinct from the *cause* of consciousness, was very similar to that of Moore. His terms are different but his meaning is much the same. He notes, for example, that the very recognition that a thing endures and is identical with itself imposes "a distinction between this essence and my intuition of it."[12] In other words, to observe that an object is the same one that was experienced earlier requires that knowing (consciousness) is one thing and the object-that-endures another.

The great difference between the pragmatists and Santayana in regard to the nature of consciousness was evidently due in large part to the fact that the former were convinced, in the light of scientific discoveries in biology and evolution, that the concept of mind as largely transcendent and contemplative must be completely abandoned, while the latter was still persuaded that, though consciousness is utterly dependent on matter and evolutionary processes for its existence, the traditional view of mind, as expressed in poetry, religion, and philosophy, is nonetheless inevitable and appropriate as an account of what mind or spirit appears to itself to be. Consciousness described in terms of physics and biopsychology, though scientifically true, he thought, is not an account of immediate experience. "Spirit refuses to be caught in a vice; it triumphs over the existence which begets it. The moving world which feeds it is not its adequate theme."[13]

A radical distinction between body and mind or matter and spirit is, he believed, therefore morally or spiritually justified—which is to say that the distinction, though false in physics and psychology, is yet necessary in order to apprehend and evaluate properly the different types and levels of human experience and activity. For matter, he claimed, "is sluggish and conservative. . . . But at each moment the wholeness of mind is spiritual and aesthetic. . . ." Consequently he saw nothing in the least anomalous or paradoxical in the fact that the individual spirit rebels at being inextricably wedded to a particular body in a particular place and time. Careful reflection, he admitted, will almost surely confirm that it is wholly irrational or absurd to suppose that one could have had a different body in another time and place and yet have been the same person. Nonetheless the distinctive attribute of the spirit is its aspiration to be free or the endeavor to see all things under the aspect of eternity—or in other words to belong essentially to no particular embodiment, place, or time. So contrary to the pragmatists, especially to James and Dewey, who thought that the dignity and worth of the mind can be found primarily if not only in its effective contributions to the solution of practical problems or to the general progress of life and civilization, Santayana insisted, "Spirit is not an instrument but a realization, a fruition. At every stage, and wherever it peeps out through the interstices of existence, it is a contemplation of eternal things."[14]

It must be emphasized, however, that the spirit's view of its own existence is not, Santayana thought, at all indicative of the actual status and character of spirit. Though spirit may seem to itself completely transcendent, ultimately, he claimed, it is simply the epiphenomenal product—a secondary, thoroughly helpless, and ephemeral result—of complex and precariously organized matter. The spirit "forms designs and develops them dramatically in idea, yet in effect it is helpless and evanescent. It awakes and dies down at no command of its own."[15] So finally spirit or consciousness is not in the least independent of the body; it only *appears* to be so. The very existence as well as many of the interests of the spirit are inseparable from the material order "because spirit is life become articulate, experience focused in thought and dominated ideally; but experience and life are inconceivable unless an organism with specific capacities and needs finds itself in an environment that stimulates it variously and offers it a conditioned career."[16]

Yet Santayana never proposed a single argument by

which the ultimate and complete dependence of consciousness on material or neural events could be rendered plausible or logically cogent. He simply found other possibilities unappealing and implausible. But whatever cogency his own view has is due no doubt in part to its very vagueness and to the fact that he himself ignored the contradictions and paradoxes implicit in it. His use of the word "matter," for example, is often so uncritical that he seems to be saying that *whatever* sustains life, spirit, and appearance is to be called *matter*. With such an approach the primacy of matter is of course so evident that one may indeed claim also that "The question, in cosmology, is not between matter and Ideas but between one sort of matter and another; and it is for experiment and science, not for logic, to discover what sort of matter matter is."[17] But is it through logic or science, by reason or experiment, that science is itself defined and the legitimacy of experiments determined? There is surely a peculiar and inescapable difficulty in the claim that the logic of science depends for its cogency on favorable events in matter. Such cogency is indeed likely to be only apparent. Furthermore, scientific experiment can hardly be sounder than the logic on which it is based. But Santayana apparently assumed, rather naively, that there is a self-evident cogency in scientific experiment, or that the logical or philosophical analysis of the methods and conditions of inquiry can never distinguish the dead ends and incompatible claims from more promising avenues and claims that are mutually supporting.

William James, though never noted for the rigor of his logic, had (guided perhaps by C. S. Peirce) seen early in his career the incongruity in the materialistic account of mind, or that the physical sciences provided an utterly inadequate basis for understanding consciousness. "Everyone," James wrote in his first major work, "admits the entire incommensurability of feeling as such with material motion as such. 'A motion became a feeling!'—no phrase that our lips can frame is so devoid of apprehensible
ness, however little, is an illegitimate birth in any philoso-
meaning."[18] A few pages later he added, "Conscious-

phy that starts without it, and yet professes to explain all facts by continuous evolution."[19] In contrast to this frank recognition of the incommensurability of "mind" and "matter" in the ordinary sense of the terms, Santayana was content to remain vague and ambiguous. His vagueness and ambiguity, as well as the radical difference between his and James's starting point, are evident in the following claim from one of his final attempts to describe his materialism: "That matter is capable of eliciting feeling and thought follows necessarily from the principle that matter is the only *substance, power,* or *agency* in the universe: and this, not that matter is the only reality, is the first principle of materialism."[20] The first part of this claim, it is clear, would be no less true regardless of the noun one might substitute for *matter. Mind, God,* or *the ether,* as one prefers, is indeed the source of all feeling and thought, *if* one names the source of all feeling and thought "God," "mind," or "the ether." But the fundamental question—Can feeling and thought be derived from nonfeeling and nonthinking substance?—has only been bypassed and clearly not answered.

Santayana was convinced that his materialism corroborated and justified his analysis of knowledge, in particular his claim that knowledge "is faith mediated by symbols,"[21] and accordingly that whatever arguments and facts supported his analysis of knowledge must also justify his materialism. This analysis of knowledge and its relations to his materialistic metaphysics will be examined in some detail in the next two chapters. It is important now, however, to indicate in summary form the major elements of what he took to be the most basic assumptions of his thought.

His philosophy began, he insisted, with "the fundamental presuppositions that I cannot live without making"; and these, he said, "are summed up in the word materialism." And this word denotes, he continued, "a great automatic engine moving out of the past into the future, not giving any reason for its being, nor any reason why I should be" and that physics alone "is competent to reveal the secret source and method of gross events, or the ways of power."[22] Yet it should be noted in this connection that Daniel Cory's "Preface" to the one-volume edition of *The Life of Reason,* published the year after Santayana's death, suggests that he was anxious to dispel the mechanistic connotations which had become attached to his materialism; he wanted, Mr. Cory said, to correct those who had so wrongly concluded that he believed "the world is composed of little wheels and springs like an enormous Swiss watch." Be this as it may, he confidently claimed that "the hereditary life of the body, modified by accident or training, forms a closed cycle of habits and actions" and that "the mind is a concomitant spiritual expression, invisible, imponderable, and epiphenomenal. . . ."[23] This is surely as mechanical in all important respects as "wheels and springs" or as any materialist hopes or any libertarian fears. However, he was perfectly willing to admit that he did not understand the process or did not know how matter can generate mind or spirit. The source of his materialism, he said, was Democritus and Lucretius among the ancients and Spinoza among the modernists.[24] Consequently he was not disturbed by the fact that there was no significant scientific support for his claims:

> Science as yet has no answer to this most important of all questions, if we wish to understand human nature, How is the body, and how are its senses and passions, determined to develop as they do? We may reply: Because God wills it so; or Because such is the character of the human species; or Because mechanical causes necessitate it. These answers do not increase our scientific understanding in the least; nevertheless they are not wholly vain: for the first tells us that we must be satisfied with ignorance; the second that we must be satisfied with the facts; and the third, which is most significant, that these facts are analogous in every province of nature.[25]

Ultimately the questions of *how* and *why* things are as they are can of course never be answered and are perhaps quite often inappropriate or devoid of genuine meaning. Yet this does not mean that every appeal to mystery is equally necessary or that our answers to ultimate questions are altogether arbitrary. Indeed the values and actions of a person can hardly be completely independent of his account of ultimate things. And one important point here is that if Santayana's account of matter and mind is accurate, then surely the contemplative spirit is completely justified in choosing detachment and reflection as the highest form of life; for in the first place it could not have chosen otherwise; but also any notion that it might by careful analysis and planning achieve more favorable results is completely illusory. For the "great automatic engine" generates but never heeds the images and ideas by which it is entertained.

But although Santayana was uncompromising in the claim that consciousness is completely dependent on organic life, and life in turn on physics and chemistry, he recognized the logical and moral difficulty in supposing that a person is identical with his body. He said, as already noted, that he could identify himself "with nothing . . . except with the flame of spirit." Accordingly, he insisted that happiness, though not independent of material necessities, mainly "resides in imaginative reflection and judgment,"[26] and that the genuine aspiration of reason is, as Aristotle claimed, "to share the vision and judgment of God" or, in more naturalistic terms, to live as much as possible in the presence of eternal truth.[27] His argument in this connection is that though the spirit is absolutely dependent on the organization of matter, "spirit is logically incomparable with body," even as the organization of matter is logically incomparable with "mere persistence or energy." Thus understood, spirit "is a moral integration and dignity accruing to body when body develops a certain degree of organization and responsiveness to distant things."[28] This seems on the one hand of course to repeat in a measure James's opinion that there is simply no "apprehensible meaning" in the claim that consciousness is a product of bodily motion, and on the other to follow the lines of Dewey's functional definition of thought. But Santayana certainly did not mean it as either. He meant instead to claim that the whole of experience confirms both the judgment that consciousness *exists* (and not simply as a function or relation) but that this existence is completely dependent on something "temporal and arbitrary,"[29] "a substance external to thought, with its parts external to one another and each a focus of existence." This substance is "the source of phenomena unsubstantial in themselves but significant of the phases of substance which produce them." This material matrix of all existence, he claimed, is also "continuous and measurable," and the transformations that occur in it are "repeated when the same conditions recur."[30] Matter is then "recondite" and the scientists are continually finding "new, wonderful, and often abstract symbols" for it; however, as *"the butt of action"* and *"the sum of all dynamic and possibly conflicting agencies in the world,"* matter, "by its motions and tensions, causes all events to take place and all appearances to appear."[31] So although it is not altogether clear just what Santayana conceived matter to be in and of itself, it is quite obvious enough that he meant to deny that it possesses any of the distinctive attributes of consciousness or spirit. He was thoroughly convinced that the organization and processes within a "dead" and "unthinking" substance somehow originate spirit when the circumstances are favorable, and that spirit or mind, although it may be said to exist, contributes nothing to the form or destiny of the complex events that occur in nature.

The great difference between Santayana and the pragmatists in regard to the character and relations of mind and matter is reflected in their different conceptions of the aim and function of philosophy. For the pragmatists philosophy must be instrumental, a way or means by which thought and ideas are effective in solving certain personal, social, and moral problems. For William James especially philosophy presumably had, as it does for the current existentialists and linguistic analysts, a certain therapeutic value; it was essentially a quite practical approach to certain speculative but nonetheless inescapable problems. And for John Dewey philosophy was basically a mode of inquiry parallel to or identical with the methods of the sciences and worthless if not an instrument in the effective control or determination of the problematic and precarious processes on which man's fortunes depend. But for Santayana philosophy was primarily contemplation and reflection—a witness to but not a causal element in events that wisdom neither attempts nor is able to control. In Santayana there was then, at least in some measure and occasionally, the Stoic ideal of philosophy as infinite resignation and complete spiritual detachment, while in pragmatism the legendary American spirit, challenged by a wilderness to be conquered and brashly confident of its own powers and resources, was clearly exemplified. For the pragmatists, therefore, philosophy and all serious thought must be an effective part of the whole; it must be a cause as well as the product of the long evolutionary struggle. Otherwise both the achievements and the goals of men are unintelligible.

In Santayana there was a profound, almost Augustinian, sense of ultimate and complete dependence: the individual spirit discovers itself a spectator of existence without the slightest notion of the struggles, the pain, the frustration, and the tragedies which accompanied the evolutionary processes by which it was presumably produced. So it seemed evident to him that mind or spirit is a consummation and not a means, a witness but in no sense or measure the director of the processes in nature. "That we are creatures and not creators," he argued, "follows from the fact that we are born to die, are dependent on matter for our very existence, and are addressed in all our passions to our transitory fortunes in the material world."[32] Dubious as each of these premises, as well as the conclusion, may be from certain other perspectives, as a whole the claim is an effective summary statement of Santayana's view of the nature and character of man's intellectual life. Mind cannot produce or sustain itself or other minds. "Ideas are not animals that may breed other animals."[33] The spirit that burns in man

—the thoughts that he thinks, the vistas that appear to him, his values, expectations, and fears—is due solely to the order and arrangement of material entities. Man lives in spite of himself; his thoughts occur spontaneously and never as the result of his own effort. Consciousness, mind, spirit—whatever name one prefers—is generated by the flux of matter, even as the colors of the rainbow are produced by the refraction of sunlight in the mist; just as the rainbow does not choose to appear and disappear, so the spirit is sustained but does not in any measure sustain or direct its own fortunes. Philosophy from this perspective is only the discipline of a spirit resigned to its own impotence but nonetheless appreciative of its undeserved capacity for knowledge and joy.

Chapter 4

ESSENCE, ACTION, AND MEANING

> "The whole rumble of the discoursing mind is music on the march, and no sane man expects it to join in battle or to describe the enemy fairly."
>
> *The Realm of Essence*

If the existence of mind or consciousness can hardly be doubted, particularly if one conceives of consciousness as a state of awareness or a function rather than an entity, the reality of various forms of *meaning* seems at least equally evident. Yet philosophers have rarely agreed about the genesis, character, function, and status of meaning. In important respects pragmatism as first formulated by C. S. Peirce and William James was primarily an attempt to solve, in the light of scientific methods and discoveries, certain difficult problems which they found in the traditional rational and empirical accounts of the nature of meaning. And no doubt George Santayana's theory of essence, at least insofar as it is also a theory of meaning, may be better understood in comparison with related themes in pragmatism. He claimed that he came to "clearness" about essence only in his old age; but in effect he separated *essence* from *existence,* as Josiah Royce noted, in his first philosophic works. Therefore his doctrine of essence will be regarded as a central element in his treatment of meaning, truth, and knowledge even in his earliest reflections on these themes.

Rationalism from Plato to the present has claimed essentially that meaning is simply anything the mind can grasp or recognize, a form, concept, or idea that is presumably independent not only of the image given in sensation or perception but also of the mind that grasps or conceives it. According to rationalism it is therefore not only possible but also necessary to comprehend *circularity,* for example, as quite independent of the particular *circle given in perception.* Indeed the clearest and most important meanings, the rationalist insists, are precisely those without any obvious counterparts in the sensory world. Number, time, love, honesty, freedom, etc., are never perceived but are conceived or grasped by the mind itself. Empiricism on the other hand, particularly since David Hume's eighteenth-century analysis of the foundations of knowledge, has insisted that all meaning consists of only two kinds: 1) those derived directly from sense experience, and 2) those that are arbitrarily determined by verbal definitions. Thus according to empiricism sense experience alone can provide a content for meaningful statements. All verbal claims not based on sensory experience are meaningless or tautological.

The American pragmatists of the late nineteenth and early twentieth centuries suggested that rationalism and empiricism are respectively too broad and too narrow in their approach to meaning. Rationalism, they said, is altogether too broad because in effect it admits that any idea, concept, experience, or figment of imagination may be genuinely meaningful; but empiricism is too narrow, they thought, in insisting that all meaning is derived ultimately from sense experience alone. The basic question at issue here may be formulated as the question of *what it is that the mind knows or apprehends* when it is said to have an idea. Does the mind know, as the rationalists claim, an idea or form that may be said to *exist* independently of both minds and the objects of sense? Or is the idea the product of an interaction between the organism and an independent physical object, as the empiricists suggested? Is what the mind knows, as Santayana claimed, an essence that cannot be said either to correspond to independent material things or to exist at all apart from its appearance? Does the mind know things themselves? Or does it know only appearances that are due ultimately to neurochemical changes in the brain?

The pragmatists were generally convinced that all genuine meaning—or what the mind knows—is somehow connected with the interests, needs, and habits of the organism that must act in order to live. In part this theory was presumably designed in order to reconcile the theory of knowledge with the Darwinian view that mind, like all the other attributes of plants and animals, is simply a product of (and does not in any measure transcend) nature. But such a view also appealed to the pragmatists because it seemed to solve the ancient and perplexing problem of the relation of mind and body, of ideas and things. If the Darwinian hypothesis were true—and the evidence apparently supporting it was enormous—the traditional view of man could be completely abandoned. The traditional view, due largely to Platonic-Judeo-Christian influence, was of course that though man is on the earth, he is not a product of it. And Newtonian science as well as religion and philosophy was based on the assumption that man, insofar as he is a mind or knower, transcends nature. Objective or genuine knowledge was presumably possible only because the world was at least in part an object *there* for man. So in the pursuit of knowledge it is not himself or his own ideas that man apprehends but an object that is presumably and completely independent of himself. But if the Darwinian view were right, man and science itself had somehow to be included in the scientific account of existence. For according to the Darwinian account man is a part of nature. So in seeking to understand nature—physics, chemistry, biology—man is at the same time seeking to know himself; and in seeking to understand himself—psychology, philosophy, politics, the arts, religion—he is also concerned to understand nature. The pragmatists saw that the radical bifurcation which had previously been possible or even inevitable between nature and man, body and mind, the subject and the object, the individual and the environment must now be completely avoided, if one wanted to be genuinely scientific. Man must fit neatly into nature and nature must be epitomized in man.

The theory of meaning developed by C. S. Peirce and William James, as well as James's claim that consciousness does not exist, was therefore designed in part to make philosophy consistent with evolutionary views. They claimed accordingly that there are no genuine meanings except those that eventuate in beliefs when belief is regarded as primarily a habit of action, or no actual difference in meaning unless some difference in action follows from it. A result of this view of course is, if it is reliable, that there is no longer any need for a sharp distinction between thought and action or mind and body. Furthermore, the puzzling and unscientific notion that thought transcends its conditions could be treated as a mistaken analysis of man's complex interests and needs. Rationalism and empiricism could now be replaced by the pragmatic claim, consistent with evolutionary theory, that meaning is basically only a product of the needs and interests of a very complicated organism seeking fulfillment in an environment that is neither wholly friendly nor completely alien to it.

Santayana was in many respects an anomaly in this context. He had, as noted already, no interest at all in making philosophy scientific—though it would be nonetheless both unfair and misleading to suggest that he thought philosophy should be either antiscientific or unscientific at its basis. Philosophy as a way of life or a "lay religion," he thought, does not need to be a scientifically true account of the way the various parts of nature fit together and influence each other. In fact he insisted that "under whatever sky" his philosophy would have been much the same. And although this claim was perhaps an exaggeration of his attitude of detachment and independence, it does indicate his evident indifference to current "winds of doctrine," whether they blew from what he regarded, so far as philosophy is concerned, as the arid deserts of the sciences or from the more pleasant and fruitful fields of the arts and religions. As a materialist he was not at all shocked by and felt no need for any significant adjustment of his own philosophical perspective because of the developing Darwinian account of the origin and nature of man. The theory of evolution was for him nothing more than the confirmation and refinement of a view that had been possible ever since the days of the first Greek materialists.

Accordingly, Santayana saw no need of modifying in the light of current developments an approach to meaning that he found, and found congenial, in the Greeks, particularly in Plato and Aristotle. His view of meaning is then almost identical with that of the rationalists. Meaning is whatever any mind happens to find meaningful; a meaning is anything that thought can grasp, recognize, identify, recall, or imagine. This infinity of meanings (or possible meanings) he called *the realm of essence*. And *essences* are different from the *ideas* of the rationalists chiefly in that, according to his account, essences cannot be said to exist. Yet as the specific character that identifies any actuality, possibility, object of thought or imagination, essences must be said to be. "They are what they are; and of all the meanings of the word *is*—existence, substance, equivalence, definition, etc., the most radical and proper is that in which I may say of anything that it is what it is."[1] An essence is then simply the character or identifiable property of anything that is or might be, whether sensory, ideal, material, or wholly imaginary. "All possible terms in mental discourse," he wrote, "are essences existing nowhere; visionary equally, whether the faculty that discovers them be sense or thought or the most fantastic fancy."[2] And emphasizing that essence is present in every form and instance of experience, he said, "I cannot read a book or think of a friend or grieve or rejoice at any fresh event, without some essence rising sensibly before me, the sole actual harvest to me of that labour."[3] Meaning then, insofar as each essence is also a meaning, is simply that which is always present in some way to consciousness.

But although Santayana accepted the rationalist theory of contemplation, as independent and determinate objects precisely by the fact that it denied the rationalist account of existence. For rationalism is committed to the claim that ideas—the objects apprehended by the mind when it considers problems of ethics as well as problems of mathematics or physics—are indeed among the inescapable *facts* of existence. Furthermore, existence is presumably a rational whole that the mind can grasp basically as it is. Of course, in certain respects Santayana acted as if essences exist; he regarded them as objects of contemplation, as independent and determinate objects of thought; but he denied, contrary to rationalism, that thought has existential implications or that reason can discover the order of existence. On the latter point he was very close to the pragmatist position. William James claimed that "Reality, life, experience, concreteness, immediacy, use what word you will, exceeds our logic, overflows and surrounds it."[4] Santayana agreed that in most respects existence is not at all amenable to logical treatment. He said in fact that logically existence is "a truly monstrous excrescence and superfluity in being. . . ."[5] The forms of existence then, far from being basically rational, are completely contingent, dependent in no sense on what is logical or reasonable but simply on the profound potentiality or dark fertility of matter—the primal accident and the mysterious matrix of all life and thought.

Yet Santayana, although close to the empiricists and the pragmatists in the view that empirical science based on observation and experiment can alone disclose something of the enduring order and habits of nature, was finally no more an empiricist or pragmatist than a rationalist in his account of the origin and nature of ideas or meanings in experience. Ever since the seventeenth century and Thomas Hobbes empiricism has claimed that there is nothing in the mind that was not first in the senses. Pragmatism insisted, however, that ideas arise primarily out of the interests, needs, and aims of men. Santayana's view was in effect less stringent than either empiricism or pragmatism. The empirical account, he thought, is too narrow because only prejudice can "suppose that experience has only such categories as colour, sound, touch, and smell." "The radical stuff of experience is much rather breathlessness, or pulsation, or as Locke said (correcting himself) a certain uneasiness; a lingering thrill, the resonance of that much-struck bell which I call my body, the continual assault of some masked enemy, masked perhaps in beauty, or of some strange sympathetic influence, like the cries and motions of other creatures." Much more important than sensory powers then "are such dichotomies as good and bad, near and far, coming and going, fast and slow, just now and very soon" or "the weight, strain, danger, and lapse of being."[6] And it is not simply needs and interests but the organism itself, he thought, that produces ideas or causes the appearance of essences. "Perceptions fall into the brain . . . as seeds into a furrowed field or even as sparks into a keg of powder. Each image breeds a hundred more, sometimes slowly and subterraneously, sometimes (when a passionate train is started) with a sudden burst of fancy." Neither reason nor perception nor need is either the chief source of ideas or ever a wholly trustworthy clue to that which exists independently of thought and perception. "The mind, exercised by its own fertility and flooded by its inner lights, has infinite trouble to keep a true reckoning of its outward perceptions."[7] There is then no necessary relation at all between what is perceived or thought and what exists. The ideas present to the mind "are like the bell-sounds heard coming from the engine-room when a steam boat stops or goes full steam ahead. The passenger, the spirit, learns very little from them about the ship, the crew, or the voyage."[8] Or in other words, "The whole life of imagination and knowledge comes from within, from the restlessness, eagerness, curiosity, and terror of the animal bent on hunting, feeding, and breeding."[9]

Thus with perfect consistency so far as the origin of ideas is concerned, Santayana defended the controversial and perhaps paradoxical doctrine that "nothing given exists."[10] He argued that what clearly exists in any instance of thought or perception is only *the experience* of some datum or essence. It is obviously a fact, he claimed, that something appears or is thought or felt in any specific experience; but that which appears or the object of thought or feeling is not also itself a fact; it does not exist.[11] The point is presumably further clarified by examples:

> Imagine a novelist whose entire life was spent in conceiving a novel, or a deity whose only function was to think a world. That world would not exist, any more than the novel would comprise the feelings and actions of existing persons. If that novelist, in the heat of invention, believed his personages real, he would be deceived: and so would that deity if he supposed his world to exist merely because he thought of it. Before the creation could be actual, or the novel historical, it would have to be enacted elsewhere than in the mind of its author.[12]

Thus thought—even if it is God thinking—Santayana suggested, in no way implies the existence of its object. Another example made essentially the same point but also emphasized the difficulty in distinguishing between thought (or imagination) and perception:

> If an angel visits me, I may intelligibly debate the question whether he exists or not. On the one hand, I may affirm that he came in through the door, that is, that he existed before I saw him; and I may continue in perception, memory, theory, and expectation to assert that he was a fact of nature: in that case I believe in his existence. On the other hand, I may suspect that he was only an event in me, called a

> dream; an event not at all included in the angel as I saw him, nor at all like an angel in the conditions of its existence; and in this case I disbelieve in my vision: for visiting angels cannot honestly be said to exist if I entertain them only in idea.[13]

And in every case, according to Santayana, whether in perception, thought, or imagination, that which appears or is present to sense or to the mind is presumably quite different in character from the existential conditions of its appearance. Essence alone appears; existence is always hidden. That the appearance as such is precisely what it appears to be is beyond doubt; but that there is an objective fact or cause of the appearance, more or less similar to it, can be only an affirmation of "animal faith," a hazardous guess or the unverifiable belief that appearance is indeed a trustworthy index to the enduring character of actual or existing objects or facts.

Is Santayana's doctrine of essence necessary or defensible? At the very least, as he noted in the final chapter and a long postscript to *The Realm of Essence,* a number of other important philosophers have also found a need for a similar category. To note some of these and their similarities and differences in comparison with Santayana's account of essence should contribute to an understanding of the problems and features of experience that seem to demand such a category as well as to a more thorough knowledge of the characteristic elements of Santayana's approach.

The basic problem, as already suggested, is to discover just what the mind knows in any instance of perception, thought, or knowledge. And there is first of all obviously some similarity between Santayana's claim that only essence or form is known and the Platonic theory of Ideas. For Plato suggested that what the mind knows is always a universal Form or Idea, more real than any concrete particular, and in some sense the cause of particulars. *Triangularity,* for instance, and not the particular triangle, said Platonism, is the only object of any genuine knowledge and the intelligible cause of the specific triangles found here and there in the world. Santayana himself observed that his theory of essence might be called "a variant of Platonism, designed to render Platonic logic and morals consistent with the facts of nature." But he immediately rejected his own suggestion and said that Platonism is not a genuine parallel to the theory of essence because Plato, in at least certain phases of his thought, turned "moral and ideal terms into supernatural powers." To regard the Idea (or an essence) as a cause, Santayana thought, is gross superstition. Consequently the similarity between his theory of essence and Platonic idealism could be defended, he noted, only insofar as by "calling his Ideas ideas and his myths myths, Plato seems to acknowledge that they are, after all, nothing but essence."[14]

Spinoza, said Santayana, was clearly aware of essence when he asserted that "every possible geometrical figure, in every possible superposition and substitution, must be equally real at every point in nature." But Spinoza was mistaken, he claimed, in supposing that the reality of such geometrical figures is indistinguishable from substance or existence. Likewise, in the philosopher Leibniz, he noted, essence appeared "under the name of 'all possible worlds' " but dropped out of sight again in an "account, credible or incredible, of some natural events and some natural existences" necessitated by a theology in which all possibilities (or essences) must be regarded as "emanations" of the mind of the Creator.[15] Thus Leibniz was thoroughly convinced that universal concepts must exist in order for the mind to apprehend or know them and that their existence was possible only as "ideas" in the mind of God. In other words, the object of thought must exist. Santayana's theory of essence denied emphatically of course that the reality of essence—eternal, passive, nonexistent, and completely ineffectual—requires anything at all as its condition; this was a corollary of the claim that the object of thought cannot be said to exist.

Santayana was apparently gratified to discover that in addition to Plato, Spinoza, and Leibniz, his own contemporaries were also preoccupied with concepts strikingly similar to his own view of essence—though again with some important differences. Among the more notable instances was Alfred North Whitehead's notion of "eternal objects," which are, however, no doubt more like Platonic Ideas than essences. But the very fact that Whitehead described them as "eternal" convinced Santayana that he was talking about essences. "Nothing," Santayana wrote, "can be more opposite to an event, or more remote from natural existence, than any eternal being."[16] He also quoted other descriptions that Whitehead applied to eternal objects as equally applicable to essences as he conceived them. "Each eternal object is an individual which, in its own peculiar fashion, is what it is." "Each eternal object is just itself, in whatever mode of realization it is involved. There can be no distortion of the individual essence without thereby producing a different eternal object." "An eternal object, such as a definite shade of green, which cannot be analysed into a relationship of components, will be called 'simple.' "[17] But the doctrine of "eternal objects," Santayana claimed, compared to the theory of essence is contaminated by a philosophic realism committed to the belief that all is reality and nothing appearance, or that everything *exists* exactly as it is experienced. And Whitehead, like Leibniz, was indeed convinced that universals cannot exist *in vacuo,* and therefore argued that the existence of God is required to provide a place, source, and sustainer for eternal objects or essences.[18] Santayana, as a thoroughgoing materialist committed to the claim that "existence is a conjunction of natures in adventitious and variable relations,"[19] had logically no alternative but to conceive essences or universals as nonexistent—since they are obviously not material and so are never involved in "adventitious and variable relations"; for all their relations are, like themselves, eternal and logically necessary. But of course to assert that essences do not exist and that the mind can know only essences is by no means to solve—but perhaps only to abandon—the basic problem of the relation between ideas and things. If what the mind knows is essence only and essence does not exist, then clearly it is only by a strange and gratuitous accident that the apprehension of essence should evidently reveal, so often and so accurately, the order and structure of things and events. This problem must be further explored in the next chapter.

As Santayana himself suggested, perhaps closest to his theory of essence among his contemporaries was the "pure phenomenology" of Edmund Husserl. Husserl himself said that *"pure or transcendental phenomenology will be established not as a science of facts, but as a science of essential Being"* and that this science "aims exclusively at establishing 'knowledge of essences.'" And like Santayana, he described essence as *nonreal* when *the real* is a synonym for *the existent. Fact* and *Essence,* he said, are terms that correspond respectively to *Real* and *not-Real.*[20] Husserl's method, Santayana observed, "consists in reducing the object to its intrinsic and evident character, disregarding all question of its existence or non-existence, or of its locus in nature; or, in my language, it consists in suspending animal faith, and living instead contemplatively, in the full intuition of some essence." This activity as such he found thoroughly congenial. But Husserl, unlike Santayana, was also convinced that a rigorous and systematic survey of phenomena (essences or appearances) will ultimately reveal not essences alone but also the order and character of the essences actually embodied in existence. Thus pure phenomenology will presumably reveal at least the structure of existence. Such phenomenology seemed both altogether too pure and too presumptive for Santayana and he labeled it "a malicious transcendentalism," suggesting, though perhaps paradoxically, that a naturalist must look "for the genesis and meaning of immediate experience," not in essences only but also "in the material and animal world."[21]

Another interesting parallel to Santayana's treatment of essence, but one about which he was evidently ignorant or indifferent, is the phenomenology of C. S. Peirce. Indeed, though Peirce and Santayana apparently took no public notice of each other, they had, in spite of wide and fundamental differences, a great deal in common. Both were realists in the sense that they believed there is, in Peirce's terms, "an external permanency" "whose characters are independent of what anybody may think them to be."[22] Peirce was, however, both more optimistic and more concerned than Santayana about the possibility of a genuine and thorough understanding of existence. This optimism was no doubt related to the fact that he was inclined to explain matter in terms of mind or that he was a panpsychist rather than a materialist.

The clearest similarities to Santayana's categories appear in an essay that Peirce called "The Principles of Phenomenology." The first point made in this essay is that there is a *phaneron* that is defined as "the collective total of all that is in any way or in any sense present to the mind, quite regardless of whether it corresponds to any real thing or not." The *phaneron* is obviously related closely to what Santayana called "the intuition of essence" or the mere presence of objects, ideas, or feelings in experience. This similarity became clearer when Peirce suggested that self-contradiction is apparently involved in the language of certain "English philosophers" who "have the habit of saying that 'there is no such idea' as this or that, in the very same breath in which they definitely describe the phaneron in question. . . ." Peirce, like Santayana, evidently means to distinguish here between that which simply *appears* to the mind (essence, meaning, phenomenon) and that which exists independently.[23]

In any account of experience, Peirce continued, three elements or modes of being may be distinguished. He called these *firstness, secondness,* and *thirdness,* indicating that they may be defined respectively as "positive qualitative possibility," "actual fact," and "law that will govern facts in the future."[24] Firstness is obviously, though not completely, identical with Santayana's essence. According to Peirce, "Firstness is the mode of being which consists in its subject's being positively such as it is regardless of aught else. That can only be possibility."[25] This is clearly a close parallel to Santayana's assertion that essences are "eternally what they are."[26] The closeness of the similarity is confirmed when Peirce added, "The mode of being a *redness,* before anything in the universe was yet red, was nevertheless a positive qualitative possibility. And redness itself, even if it be embodied, is something positive and *sui generis.*"[27] And although Santayana eventually insisted that " 'possible' and 'impossible' have . . . no proper application in the realm of essence,"[28] this was due largely to the fact that he used the terms in a narrower sense than Peirce did. For Peirce "possible" apparently meant, as Santayana admitted it sometimes may, "the materially impossible, provided it is imaginable."[29] Furthermore, Baker Brownell has claimed that his lecture notes show that from 1910–1912 Santayana "did identify essence with possibility. He emphasized it strongly in his lectures and often called essence the realm of possibility. He changed his position on this later."[30] In any case Peirce clearly never intended to claim that *redness,* apart from the "actual fact" of eyes and light rays, is an actual possibility or that unicorns are possibilities in the same sense that hybrids such as mules are. Yet, not being a materialist, Peirce was perhaps not as certain as Santayana apparently was that a genuine distinction is always possible or necessary between actual and merely logical possibilities. Nonetheless both Peirce, with the concept of firstness, and Santayana, with essence, may be said to have identified the infinite modes or forms of being, distinct from actual existence, that may be distinguished as a specific this or that. Or in other words both were apparently convinced that the realm of meaning is infinitely greater than the realm of existence.

There is also a notable similarity between Peirce's concept of *secondness* or "actual fact" and Santayana's *realm of matter.* Peirce suggested that "facts are proverbially called brutal" because "we feel facts resist our will. Now mere qualities do not resist. It is the matter that resists."[31] Quality then, like essence, is immaterial and inactive; and fact, like matter, resists, acts, and reacts. In a very close parallel, Santayana said, "The realm of matter, from the point of view of our discovery of it, is the field of action: it is essentially dynamic and not pictorial." But he departed significantly from Peirce's view when he added, "From the point of view of origins, therefore, the realm of matter is the matrix and source of everything: it is nature, the sphere of genesis, the universal mother."[32] It would be more nearly correct, according to Peirce, to say that thought is the only imaginable source of either intelligence or an intelligible world. So the profound difference between the two is that Santayana insisted that finally consciousness, spirit, or thought is simply a product of material organization and process while Peirce was convinced that matter itself, with its intelligible order and processes, must be understood as a form of primitive or "effete mind." And this difference is perhaps better evident in Peirce's treatment of *thirdness.*

Thirdness, Peirce said, "we call laws when we contemplate them from the outside only, but which when we see both sides of the shield we call thoughts."[33] This claim points at once to both the fact that *law,* as Peirce understood it, is not, as Santayana thought, merely imputed by an observer to adventitious regularities that appear in nature, and that mind (spirit, thought, consciousness), as Peirce regarded it, cannot be a "superfluous" or "epiphenomenal" event so far as the total order and process of nature is concerned. For Peirce law is a definite "sign" of the presence of "thought" in nature, and man's mind is a reflection or recognition of the "meaning" that pervades and determines existence and not, as Santayana supposed, the gratuitous product of the organism itself. Peirce claimed, in his own words, that "the idea of meaning is irreducible to those of quality and reaction" or, in Santayana's terms, that thought cannot be simply a product of essence and matter. Meaning, said Peirce, always involves "a triadic relation," or a sign, the signified, and "some interpretant thought."[34] "Just as action requires a peculiar kind of subject, matter, which is foreign to mere quality, so law requires a peculiar kind of subject, the thought, or, as the phrase in this connection is, the mind, as a peculiar kind of subject foreign to mere individual action."[35] Laws, he consequently suggested without any inconsistency, might be regarded as "thoughts" in the mind of God, except that it is unscientific and unphilosophic to appeal to God. But the most relevant point could hardly be more clear: the assumption made by Santayana that material processes in complex organisms, resulting in the apprehension of eternal and inert essences, are the foundation of all experience and knowledge, is not one that other thinkers have generally been able to share. But whether their insight or their illusion has been more profound than his only further inquiry can hopefully determine.

In summary, Santayana shared the concern of his contemporaries for the problem of meaning; and he agreed with those who distinguished sharply between the problem of meaning on the one hand and the problem of existence and knowledge on the other. Unlike the pragmatists and in common with the long tradition of the rationalists, he denied that meaning is exclusively or even basically a reflection of the problems and perplexities of man's existential situation. He agreed with the rationalists that thought transcends its own conditions, that the spirit may contemplate the eternal and is frequently indifferent to the solution of the most practical and urgent problems. But unlike the rationalists, he attached no existential significance to the essences, eternal objects, forms, or ideals that the spirit may apprehend and contemplate. That which appears to sense or thought is presumably appearance only. And appearances "possess intrinsically, in their own ontological plane, only logical or aesthetic being; and this contains no indication whatever of the material act of speaking, touching, or looking which causes them to appear."[36] His concept of meaning is thus infinitely broader or more inclusive than the empirical and pragmatic theories of meaning. For although empiricism admits that the mind may combine the elements derived from sense in unprecedented ways—and that consequently such nonexistent entities as golden mountains, unicorns, werewolfs, and mermaids are "meaningful" concepts, although nothing true can be asserted about them—it also claims there is nothing in the mind that was not first in sense. Santayana admitted no such limits to what may be meaningfully given in thought or imagination. His doctrine of essence is in part precisely a denial of the empirical account of the origin and nature of ideas. For the doctrine of essence assumes that there is no demonstrable or actual relation at all between what is experienced or thought and what exists.

The character and significance of the claim that meanings do not exist may perhaps be further clarified by a very brief comparison with the views of John Dewey. "Meanings," said Dewey, "are taken; they are employed for a purpose, just as other materials are; they are combined and disjoined. . . . Using meanings is a particular act. . . . The existence of error is proof, not disproof, of the fact that all meanings intrinsically have reference to natural events."[37] Even though Dewey's approach is perhaps extreme also in its own way, it is helpful here because a view could hardly be more directly opposed to Santayana's account of essence as meaning. Meanings are not used, he insisted; they are only known, grasped, and contemplated; they may or may not apply to natural events. In any case, he thought, it can ultimately be only by a lucky accident that sense or thought discovers the character of any actual thing or process. For the fact that a person apprehends the essences that he does apprehend—that he thinks the thoughts he happens to think—is never due to the intention or self-originated effort of the man himself. Instead, both his intention and his thought are due alike to the blind flux of matter—to its changing order and organization—within him. Meanings (essences) are eternal; but those that occur to a particular individual at a particular time and place are due only to the material forces that produce and sustain him, and not in the least to his own aims or efforts. In such a framework the pursuit of truth in any rigorous sense of the term is of course largely impossible and irrelevant. Santayana's view of truth is therefore the chief theme of the next chapter.

Chapter 5

ACTION, KNOWLEDGE, AND TRUTH

". . . and the more clearly we perceive the inevitable, all-comprehensive, eternal being of truth, the more improbable or even impossible must seem the notion that any human conception should ever do it justice."

The Realm of Truth

Like all claims that distinguish sharply between appearance and reality or ideas and things, George Santayana's claim that experience is always of essences which do not exist raises enormous problems for any serious attempt to separate "fact" from "fantasy" or "truth" from "imagination" and "illusion." Indeed it might be argued that he was not seriously interested in truth, that his philosophy articulated by choice only certain imaginary "perfections" rather than the "hard facts" of existence. In some measure he would himself concur in such a judgment. In his very first philosophical book, *The Sense of Beauty,* he wrote that "unless human nature suffers an inconceivable change, the chief intellectual and aesthetic value of our ideas will always come from the creative action of the imagination."[1] Again, in the middle of his career, in "A Brief History of My Opinions," he addressed himself directly to the question of the values of life and reaffirmed the conviction that the products of the imagination "are good, they alone are good; and the rest—the whole real world—is ashes in the mouth."[2] And in the first volume of his autobiography, published after he was eighty years old, he reviewed his dominant approach to life in very similar terms: "According to my youthful heart, existence was profoundly ugly and wrong. The beautiful remained imaginary. . . . That the real was rotten and only the imaginary at all interesting seemed to me axiomatic. . . . My philosophy has never changed."[3] Such a mind, confronting the perplexities in the pursuit of truth, can perhaps tolerate the most glaring contradictions and ambiguities.

Yet a philosopher—even though he may regard himself as a nonprofessional—can hardly avoid all serious attempts to evaluate in terms of their validity and truth his own claims and systems as well as the claims and systems of others. Perhaps the most forthright, if not the most candid and revealing, instance of self-evaluation by Santayana occurred early in *The Realm of Truth.* The result was perhaps consistent with the claim that the products of the imagination are finally more important than truth:

> A rationalistic reader might . . . ask: "Is there no truth within your realm of essence? Are not unity and distinctness present in all essences, and is it not true to say so? And all that you yourself have written, here and elsewhere, about essence, is it not true?" No, I reply, it is not true, nor meant to be true. It is a grammatical or possibly a poetical construction having, like mathematics or theology, a certain internal vitality and interest; but in the direction of truth-finding, such constructions are merely instrumental like any language or any telescope. . . . But logic is only logic: and the systems of relation discoverable amongst essences do not constitute truths, but only more comprehensive essences, within which the related essences figure as parts. The systems, like the logical elements, become a means of expressing truth only when truth can be otherwise discovered and brought face to face with our deductive reasonings.[4]

He of course claimed to have no way of bringing truth "face to face" with reason; and he clearly did not wish to defend the *truth* of his claims about the various realms of being. But although this self-evaluation may be consistent with the claim that the products of the imagination are better and more important than truth, such an account of his own aims and achievements is nonetheless paradoxical. If indeed it is true, as the theory of essence presumably implies, that "nothing given exists," then surely the approach to truth must be more limited and altogether different from what it should be if the mind can know fact as well as appearance; it is still necessary, however, as Santayana sometimes recognized, to assume that the truth can in some respects be known and stated. Consequently it seems not only appropriate but also necessary to assume that Santayana, in spite of occasional disclaimers, was quite seriously concerned, among other things, to articulate the truth about at least certain important aspects of existence. He in fact acknowledged that "A philosopher cannot wish to be deceived," that "The pursuit of truth is a form of courage, and a philosopher may well love truth for its own sake, in that he is disposed to confront destiny, whatever it may be, with zest when possible, with resignation when necessary, and not seldom with amusement."[5] Although he himself apparently valued certain other things more than he valued knowledge of the truth, he also recognized that in order to live wisely or well one needs to know in some measure and in some respects "what sort of world this disturbing world happens to be."[6]

Again Santayana's views, in both their origin and their import, may be better understood in comparison with the views of his contemporaries, particularly the claims and arguments of the men who were his teachers and his colleagues at Harvard. He disagreed most consciously and emphatically with the idealistic rationalism of Josiah Royce. Royce as an idealist was committed to the claim that existence must be a rational whole and that truth is known in proportion to the consistency and completeness of the system of ideas through which the facts and relations of experience are expressed or interpreted. Appearance or illusion is the fragmentary, the incomplete, the incoherent or disjointed. The problem of truth is then basically a logical problem. "The world is the interpretation of the problems which it presents."[7] In this account truth is not a function of empirical verification but of consistent or logical thought. "A man who sees a photograph sees truth, if he is intelligent enough to observe it. A man who sings a tune sings truth, if he is thoughtful enough to know what he is doing."[8] Thus the thought or interpretation is the element of importance. To be true is simply to be. "To be," however, "means simply to express, to embody the complete internal meaning of a certain absolute system of ideas,—a system, moreover, which is genuinely implied in the true internal meaning or purpose of every finite idea, however fragmentary."[9] In a world that is itself a "system of ideas" the very character and the only purpose of thought is to discover and know the truth.

But more influential and challenging than the views of Royce, particularly to philosophic inquiry in the first half of the twentieth century, was the pragmatic account of the nature of truth. C. S. Peirce conceived pragmatism originally as essentially a *method* of inquiry and proof. But he recognized that a method has implications for the nature of existence and the truth that can be discovered about it. He defined "truth" as "the character of a proposition which consists in this, that belief in the proposition *would,* with sufficient experience and reflection, lead us to such conduct as *would* tend to satisfy the desires we should then have."[10] But it must be emphasized that "the desires we should then have" would be due to our recognition of the actual nature of existence. In other words, according to Peirce, truth is public; it is that which anyone with the attitude of "a dweller in a laboratory" will believe if he carries his inquiries and reflections far enough. The truth is discovered, according to Peirce, by the convergence and agreement of independent minds on an "external permanency" that it is what it is regardless of what anyone happens to think about it. Thus the *truth* may be said to be that to which the community of scientific investigators is "fated" to agree.

Certain important similarities between the views of Peirce and Santayana have already been noted. But it was of course the pragmatism of William James that Santayana knew best, was most influenced by, and in some measure deliberately rejected. Although James admitted the originality of Peirce and his own debt to him, his own views were significantly different. He was never tempted, for better or worse, to suppose that truth demands exclusively the attitude and method of "the dweller in a laboratory." Consequently he reflected better than Peirce perhaps the radical pluralism—or the ultimate reality of individuals—which both regarded as a basic characteristic of existence. He was also more keenly aware of the apparent influence of the knower and his instruments—of man's needs and his language—in the processes of knowing. This may mean that James was simply too much involved with the personal problems of himself and others to believe that the dispassion and objectivity Peirce sought were really possible. In any case "truth" for James was primarily a function of experience, not a character or quality of propositions or language. Truth then need not be *about* an "external permanency"; it need not be eternal or objective. "Truth is made, just as health, wealth, and strength are made, in the course of experience."[11] So truth, according to James, is what guides man in the attempt to satisfy his various needs. The truth may then sometimes refer to a supposed "external permanency"—the chemicals in a test tube, for example—that is presumably unaffected by any thought of it. But the truth may also be an expression of individual needs and desires, the demands of character and aspiration, the envisagement of possibilities that would not exist apart from the individual. Truth may belong to belief simply by virtue of the fact that it is (or seems to be) necessary in order to justify moral action or to make life worth living. There may be, James admitted, no external permanency whatever. But the truth still is. For truth is whatever guides the individual through "the aboriginal sensible muchness" of existence or through the welter of experienced qualities, quantities, relations, and meanings that compose the world that man knows.

Santayana's account of experience and existence made

it impossible for him to be either a rationalist or a pragmatist in his account of what the truth is. For although he agreed with Peirce that there is an external world unaffected by thought about it, he could conceive of no way in which this world could be reliably discovered and described by man. Mere coherence in thought or dialectic, he insisted, indicates in itself nothing at all about the existence or structure of the world of fact. "The dialectical world would be a trackless desert if the existent world had no arbitrary constitution."[12] Any of a number of rational or coherent worlds, he claimed, are equally possible and may be imagined while the actual world exhibits undeniable signs of incoherence and absurdity. Therefore, "To reduce truth to coherence is to deny truth, and to usurp that name for a certain comfort and complacency in mere thinking."[13] Rationalism, he believed, failed to make an absolutely necessary distinction between the character of thought and the ultimate character of nonmental existence.

Santayana made equally unsympathetic comments about certain pragmatic doctrines. "If an 'idea' is useful," he wrote, "it is useful, not true: if an idea is beautiful and comforting, it is not therefore true, but comforting only or beautiful."[14] He recalled in "A General Confession" that in spite of James's earlier influence on him, the book on *Pragmatism* gave him "a rude shock" and that he "could not stomach that way of speaking about truth." Yet he acknowledged in the very same pages that his own philosophy included "a sort of pragmatism." What he apparently recognized as pragmatic was his claim that the value of ideas is always only "symptomatic, expressive, and symbolic," and that such ideas are "rational partly by their vital and inward harmony—for reason is a harmony of the passions—and partly by their adjustment to external facts and possibilities—for reason is a harmony of the inner life with truth and with fate." Or expressed in slightly different terms, pragmatism entered his thought, he suggested, in the form of the claim that "The human mind is a faculty of dreaming awake, and its dreams are kept relevant to its environment and to its fate only by the external control exercised over them by Punishment, when the accompanying conduct brings ruin, or by Agreement, when it brings prosperity."[15] There is indeed a very close parallel between these claims and the pragmatist conviction that the truth is that which *works* or that which *guides* men in the fulfillment of their needs and desires. And James was no doubt the chief spokesman for this doctrine. But Dewey was willing to say only that truth is "an agreement of existence and mind or thought" insofar as the correspondence or agreement is "like that between an invention and the conditions which the invention is intended to meet." "The agreement, correspondence, is between purpose, plan, and its own execution, fulfillment; between a map of a course constructed for the sake of guiding behavior and the result attained in acting upon the indications of the map."[16] Santayana agreed that much of the value of ideas is pragmatic in this sense.

But insofar as the pragmatists were also convinced that action, experiment, or successful practice reveals the very character of existence as distinguished from experience itself, Santayana was no pragmatist. He defined "the truth" as "the complete ideal description of existence" and added that "any part of this description will be a truth, that is a part of the truth."[17] Truth is then constituted precisely of those nonexisting essences that happen to be also embodied in existence. Therefore the *knowledge of truth* can be only *the presence* to some mind of the *exact essences* embodied in existence together with the *belief* that just those essences are in fact exemplified in things and relation. *Belief* is required because the mind or experience never witnesses existence as such. And accordingly men do not for the most part know the truth. "Men are ruled by imagination: imagination makes them into men, capable of madness and of immense labours. We work dreaming. . . . What saves us is the fact that our imaginations, groundless and chimerical as they may seem, are secretly suggested and controlled by shrewd old instincts of our animal nature, and by continual contact with things."[18] Things are not indeed what they appear to be. "Knowledge is accordingly belief,"[19] "animal faith," or the assumption, impossible to verify, that what is present to the mind—whether in perception, thought, or imagination—is also indicative of the world of actual objects that exist independently. Certainty in regard to truth is impossible precisely because there is no way to ascertain how close the similarity is between the essences the mind apprehends, that are the objects of belief, and the actual objects they must resemble in order for beliefs to be true. True knowledge is impossible—if by knowledge one means the certainty that existing things have one character rather than another. For "knowledge is a name for the effects which surrounding things" may have on an organism stimulated by them,[20] and so in all knowledge "there must be some such thing as a justified illusion, an irrational pretension by chance fulfilled, a chance shot hitting the mark."[21]

Perhaps the basic difference between Santayana and the pragmatists is that he was unwilling to equate *knowledge* and *truth*. "Knowledge is not truth," he wrote, "but a view or expression of the truth; a glimpse of it secured by some animal with special organs under special circumstances."[22] Although he often expressed contempt for the pragmatic theory of truth, his own approach to *knowledge of truth* (as distinct from his conviction about *what the truth is)* must, however, be described as thoroughly pragmatic. He asserted that "The images in sense are parts of discourse, not of nature: they are the babble of our innocent organs under the stimulus of things." This may seem a denial of the pragmatic notion that perceptions and ideas serve essentially to meet the needs of the organism. But he added on the same page that the images of sense "may become signs, if discourse is intelligent and can recapitulate its phases, for the things sought or encountered in the world."[23] Belief is accordingly defined in thoroughly pragmatic terms: "Ideas become beliefs only when by precipitating tendencies to action they persuade me that they are signs of things."[24] In *The Realm of Truth* he indicated more fully the sense in which he regarded images and ideas as "signs of things." "An animal vision of the universe is, in one sense, never false: it is rooted in the nature of that animal, aroused to consciousness by the circumstances of the moment."[25] The "truth" in such animal vision, if "nothing given exists," however, can clearly be only its reliability as a guide to action or to the fulfillment of vital and spiritual needs, to the opportunities and dangers within the environment. So although he insisted that it is an illusion to suppose "that scientific ideas reveal the literal and intimate essence of reality, as the images of sense certainly do not," he also claimed that in fact "both sense and science are relatively and virtually true, being appropriate to the organ employed and to the depth to which this organ may penetrate into the structure of things or may trace their movement."[26] Therefore it seems obvious that the only possible function of sense and science—except as they may provide imaginary and pleasant vistas for contemplation—is to reflect the character of things *insofar as these are relative to the instruments and needs of man.* And certainly these are thoroughly pragmatic functions, even though man's interests and needs, as Santayana conceived them, are by no means as narrowly practical as the views so often (though no doubt sometimes erroneously) attributed to pragmatism would imply.

There is then evidently no great gulf between Santayana's claim that man must trust sense and science as the servants of his interests even though no truth about actual things is discovered by them and James's claim that the truth is what can be verified by its results or Dewey's insistence that a true idea is one that serves as an instrument for solving specific problems. All these views are based alike upon the premise that needs and interests, related to particular instruments and powers, determine both the fact and the character of knowledge. They are equally far from the more optimistic rationalist claim that the order of thought is also the order of existence and the historically recurring theme, lately emphasized by existentialists such as Martin Heidegger, that man is in certain respects at least an "openness" to existence. Nonetheless it must be emphasized that Santayana's scepticism about the possibility of genuine knowledge was much more thoroughgoing than that of either James or Dewey. In respect to certain traditional methods and claims—particularly the procedures and premises of the rationalistic and religious approaches to truth—it is quite appropriate to regard James and Dewey as *sceptics*. Yet James sometimes appeared almost incredibly naive and credulous in regard to the existential implications of certain ideas and experiences. And Dewey sometimes seemed to share all the shallow optimism of certain nineteenth-century thinkers in respect to the possibility of completely understanding and controlling nature, including man and society, through the careful use of the scientific method. James perhaps expressed the essential and also the best element of pragmatism when he said, "To copy a reality is, indeed, one very important way of agreeing with it, but it is far from being essential. The essential thing is the process of being guided."[27] For both James and Dewey the truth of an idea is related basically and necessarily to its function as a guide through the problematics of the human situation. Yet Dewey especially thought that science has proved its unparalleled superiority as a method of being guided. Santayana, however, emphasized that there is an immense difference between the utility and the truth of an idea and that in some respects science cannot be finally any more trustworthy than the senses or the arts and religions. "Ultimately," he said, "the authority of science will always depend on the evidence of sense and on the analogy of familiar objects and events."[28] And if "nothing given exists," if the senses apprehend only essence and not existence, science is therefore always at least one remove from any genuine acquaintance with or account of the actual facts. Its *truth* is genuinely but thoroughly functional and human. And in this sense, he clearly thought, the arts and religions may also be said to be true. For after all, "The conditions and the aims of life are both represented in religion poetically"; and although "this poetry tends to arrogate to itself literal truth and moral authority, neither of which it possesses,"[29] religion may still be said to be a guide to certain moral and spiritual fulfillments. And if it is perhaps more accurate to say that he regarded religions as "better or worse, never true or false,"[30] it is nonetheless the case that he used "truth" and "falsity" in the attempt to indicate the genuine and important place of religion in the life of reason: "The only truth of religion comes from its interpretation of life, from its symbolic rendering of that aspiration which it springs out of and which it seeks to elucidate. Its falsehood comes from the insidious misunderstanding which clings to it, to the effect that these poetic conceptions are not merely poetical, but are literal information about experience or reality elsewhere. . . ."[31]

There are then finally at least three important differences in emphasis between Santayana and the pragmatists in respect to knowledge and truth. First, as already suggested, the pragmatists, like the traditional empiricists, were inclined to suppose that existence is what man's experience—his interests, his problems, the ways of fulfilling his needs, however, rather than sense experience alone—suggests it is. Pragmatic assumptions and methods, they seemed to believe, are indeed ways of knowing the actual character of existence. Santayana was convinced that this is not the case at all. What existence is in itself, as distinguished from experience, he was convinced that man will never know. Interests and needs, he thought, reveal only that man has such interests and needs, and any particular fulfillment does not preclude the possibility of others equally satisfying but utterly different in their existential implications. One is therefore the victim of illusion, he claimed, if he supposes that existence ever really has the character that human interests and needs attribute to it; one might as well suppose that existence is most truly revealed to the eye of the peacock or the interests of the tiger. He ridiculed the notion that pragmatism is a way of discovering the truth by an imaginative account of the "spontaneous pragmatism" of a president of a state university "obliged to defend the study of Sanskrit before a committee of senators. 'You have been told,' he would say, 'that Sanskrit is a dead language. Not at all: Sanskrit is Professor Smith's department, and growing. The cost is trifling, and several of our sister universities are making it a fresh requirement for the Ph.D. in classics. That, gentlemen, is what Sanskrit is.' "[32]

The second important difference is that the pragmatists, again as already noted, were also inclined to interpret man's interests and needs as more narrowly practical than Santayana was ready to grant. James thought, for example, that religion in order to be important must be somehow practical; and if it is practical, he seemed at least to argue, religion must be true. On the other hand Dewey thought that since religion is so obviously impractical—because of its inordinate demands on time and energies that might be more profitably used—it cannot possibly be regarded as true. Santayana was convinced that this approach mistook the means for the ends of existence and valued life for the wrong reasons. That religion or the arts should be conceived as basically instrumental, or as useless unless they are practical and true, he found shocking and completely unacceptable. Contemplation or the free life of the mind, he thought, is the chief justification of existence; and from this perspective religion and the arts appeared to belong, regardless of their lack of utility, among the very highest achievements of man.

Thus the third significant difference in comparison with the pragmatists is that Santayana was not as inclined as they (and others) were to value the truth either for its own sake or for its practical results. The great concern to know the truth no matter how ugly or unpleasant the truth is—although he admitted it as a legitimate goal of the mind—seemed to him in certain respects both futile and tragic: futile because it is impossible to reach the truth as such and tragic because it distracts men from more reasonable and attainable values. This view is no doubt responsible in large part for the widespread tendency to suppose that Santayana was not an altogether serious philosopher or that he did not regard the human predicament as seriously as did the pragmatists and most other philosophers. Justified as this conclusion may in part be, it is not the whole truth. Certainly Santayana was convinced that preoccupation with the pursuit of truth, and particularly the fanatical defense of certain dogmatic versions of it, is essentially a form of madness. And the proper aim of the intellect, he clearly believed, is not an unattainable truth. Indeed, more luck than insight or purpose is involved, he thought, if the truth is found and is responsible for felicitous results. "Happiness in the truth is like happiness in marriage, fruitful, lasting, and ironical. You could not have chosen better, yet this is not what you dreamt of."[33] The good and the beautiful are more important and more attainable than truth. "Truth cannot dictate to love. . . . Nearer and lovelier things also solicit us. We must turn to them; yet not without a constant speculative reverence for the truth in its divine immensity."[34] So the highest and genuine function of the mind is not to discover the truth but "rather to increase the wealth of the universe in the spiritual dimension, by adding appearance to substance and passion to necessity, and by creating all those private perspectives, and those emotions of wonder, curiosity, and laughter which omniscience would exclude."[35] If this is not serious enough or sufficiently concerned about the terrible perplexities and predicaments of man, he could also write, "The great characteristic of the human spirit, as I see it, is its helplessness and misery, most miserable and helpless when it fancies itself dominant and independent; and the great problem for it is salvation, purification, rebirth into an humble recognition of the powers on which it depends, and into a sane enjoyment of its appropriate virtues."[36]

To aim primarily at either understanding (truth) or the more practical goal of controlling the environment is, he thought, to deny the ultimate dependence of man on powers that are infinite and indeed unknowable. The only reasonable aim, he suggested, is the cultivation of the life of the mind or spirit, a transcendence of the world "by transmuting it into terms of art, of love and of reflection."[37] He scorned the pragmatist approach to truth because he disagreed with pragmatic interests and aims or because it seemed clear to him that the pragmatists were really concerned about impossible goals; for it seemed to him that they were primarily concerned to control or manipulate nature, or (in the case of James particularly) about psychological adjustment and comfort, or about panaceas and miraculous remedies that neither enlighten the human spirit about its predicaments nor entertain it with more congenial perspectives. To take seriously the view that man's needs are exclusively practical, or that following practical interests will make life worth living, he insisted, is as unrealistic or illusory as the supposition that interests and needs reveal nature as it is in itself. Man cannot live, he believed, without illusions; and so illusions are not as such either irrelevant or undesirable. What hinders and frustrates the spirit, he claimed, is therefore not illusion as such but the mistake of supposing that the illusion is itself the truth.

There is hardly a better summary of Santayana's attitude towards the possibility of knowing the truth than the rhetorical question in the final lines of his novel, *The Last Puritan:* "After life is over and the world has gone up in smoke," he asked, "what realities might the spirit in us still call its own without illusion save the form of these very illusions which have made up our story?" Experience is the presence to the senses or to the mind or spirit of essences, or the presence of forms of appearance that do not exist at all except as the result of occasional events in some brain. Since the presence of particular essences is due finally to material events, to molecular processes and arrangements in the body, there is no more reason to assume that experience as given resembles that which exists independent of experience than there is to suppose that the colors and forms of the rainbow resemble the particles of water and the light waves that they presumably refract. That which exists and that which appears are, he thought, at least so far as is known, utterly different from each other. Knowledge is then simply true belief—a belief that experience does indeed reflect the essences embodied in existence. The problem of course is that there is no way to get beyond experience or to compare the essence given in appearance with the essences exemplified in the world of fact. Ultimately then no form of experience—sensory, dialectical, scientific, religious, or artistic—can be trusted as a genuine mode of discovering the truth about existence or even as a way of fulfilling man's hopes and desires. The claims and promises of all the forms of experience are equally in need of being purified by disillusion—or by the conviction that the only way not to be deceived is "to entertain the illusion without succumbing to it, accepting it openly as an illusion, and forbidding it to claim any sort of being but that which it obviously has; and then, whether it profits me or not, it will not deceive me."[38]

Santayana's admission that there is nothing inconsistent or self-contradictory in the claim of the solipsist that the entire external world is the product of his own imagination or thought is then quite compatible with the main themes of his philosophic theory. For surely if the mere belief that some appearances are indicative of existence is the chief or only distinction between the themes of knowledge and the themes of imagination, there can obviously be no assurance that the entire panorama before me is other than the product of my own fancy—or brain, except that the solipsist who is also a materialist and an epiphenomenalist cannot consistently affirm the existence of his own brain. Even though beliefs are defined as the willingness to act on certain signs, such willingness also *seems* to occur in dreams. There is, however, the same basic difficulty in Santayana's approach to truth that he attributes to the solipsist. The solipsist, he notes, can have no enduring reason for believing his own claims. Solipsism can be consistent only as long as it is confined to the present moment and not seriously defended.[39] Similarly the claim that truth is impossible except as the belief (or faith) that certain experiences, because they inspire actions, are trustworthy clues to existence, cannot be consistently conceived or derived as the conclusion to a sound argument. For a claim that dismisses the possibility of truth is not only peculiarly ambitious but also paradoxical because to know that experience is illusory, that the given does not exist, is presumably to stand in the presence of an important truth with extraordinary implications. And although one cannot perhaps prove the existence of God, as Josiah Royce thought one could, from the mere fact of error, surely the man who knows he is deceived must have some enduring standard of truth, no matter how ill-conceived, against which he can measure his own deception.

Chapter 6

DETERMINISM AND TELEOLOGY

> "Nature is full of coiled springs and predestined rhythms; of mechanisms so wound up that, as soon as circumstances permit, they unroll themselves through a definite series of phases."
>
> *The Realm of Matter*

The problem of determinism and teleology, of cause and purpose, is indeed one of the more persistent and thorny of philosophical issues. Whether all events are caused by the blind and aimless concatenation of things according to inexorable law, or whether "some idea, seen under the form of the good," must "guide and attract every movement in nature?" may be here regarded as a convenient (though incomplete) form of the question. George Santayana agreed that the latter is "the normal way of speaking." He added, however, that this is a "rhetorical or poetical way of describing nature in human terms from the human point of view,"[1] meaning that this account is not actually or "literally" true. Yet he was also unwilling to grant that what is usually called a deterministic description of events is wholly correct. For the "so-called" "physical or dialectical laws" in terms of which such descriptions must be made, he said, are really only "rash generalisations" that lead the "stupid but learned—not a rare combination—" "to think that everything must necessarily happen as the men of science, or the philosophies of history, explain that it happens. . . ." And this, he continued, is not so very different from the belief of the "stupid and ignorant" who conclude that everything has "to be as it is at home; that there could be no good language, religion, or taste other than their own."[2] Thus he denied in significant respects both the traditional teleological and the deterministic descriptions of nature; and his attempt to construct a comprehensive view of existence without taking seriously such concepts as law, choice, freedom, cause, and purpose is accordingly one of the most notable features, if not also one of the more serious faults, of his philosophical perspective. His ambiguity and his radical differences from other thinkers in respect to such concepts were perhaps due in part to the poetic and reflective character of his thought, as most of his critics would readily agree; but they were evidently due also to the genuine problems and conflicts in both the relevant experience and then current formulations of the issues as well as to other basic assumptions of his own philosophy.

In the latter half of the nineteenth century science, whether physics or biology, and the philosophies influenced by it were generally deterministic or based on the assumption of the invariable and complete applicability of the "law of causality" to every event in nature, including human thought and behavior. A classic statement of the theory as then held is found in the *Logic* of John Stuart Mill:

> The state of the whole universe at any instant, we believe to be the consequence of its state at the previous instant; insomuch that one who knew all the agents which exist at the present moment, their collocation in space, and all their properties, in other words, the laws of their agency, could predict the whole subsequent history of the universe. . . . And if any particular state of the entire universe could

ever recur a second time, all subsequent states would return too, and history would, like a circulating decimal of many figures, periodically repeat itself.[3]

A view very similar to this, and one with which C. S. Peirce and William James must have been well acquainted, was defended by the American philosopher, Chauncey Wright. Wright was one of the leading intellects of the age, a member of the Metaphysical Club of Cambridge, a loosely organized philosophical forum that included Peirce and James. "The very hope of experimental philosophy," said Wright, "its expectation of constructing the sciences into a true philosophy of nature, is based on the induction, or, if you please, the a priori presumption, that physical causation is universal." Yet the profound difficulty and the conflict involved in this issue are indicated by the fact that Wright found it necessary to claim that Darwin had "undoubtedly erred" because he had not "repeated with sufficient frequency his faith in the universality of the law of causation. . . ." Darwin had not pointed out often enough, he explained, "that in referring any effect to 'accident,' he only means that its causes are like particular phases of the weather, or like innumerable phenomena in the concrete course of nature generally, which are quite beyond the power of finite minds to anticipate or to account for in detail, though none the less really determinate or due to regular causes."[4] To many others, however, it was by no means clear that Darwin either had or could afford to appeal to "physical causation" exclusively, and the theory of evolution was at least one of the reasons that certain other thinkers abandoned determinism.

The emphasis on the physical as the matrix of all causes, though not the principle of causality in its most deterministic form, was of course to become a basic thesis in the thought of Santayana. But neither the physical matrix nor the principle of causality was acceptable to the pragmatists. C. S. Peirce identified three basic flaws in the deterministic account of things and events.[5] (He formulated five arguments against "the doctrine of necessity," as he called it; but two of his arguments apparently rest on the same or very similar characteristics of nature; and the fifth is a purported mathematical discovery or scheme that he never made public.) His first important argument applied chiefly to the emphasis on "physical causation." Any determinism conceived in terms of physical causation alone, he argued, is a *reductio ad absurdum* in the sense that neither the order of nature (or its intelligibility) nor consciousness (or intelligence) can be at all explained or understood in such terms. Within the context of physical determinism, he claimed, mind or consciousness inevitably becomes "a mere illusory aspect of a material system." In the resulting world neither intelligence nor purpose, and so neither explanation nor personal choice, can have any truly significant or efficient place. Thus Peirce insisted that the view Santayana defended, that mind is epiphenomenal and ephemeral, is the logical but nonetheless absurd and paradoxical consequence of the assumption that the matrix of all causes is physical.

Peirce's second argument applies equally to all forms of determinism and not simply to the view that all causation is physical. This argument is that growth and spontaneity, which he regarded as among the most evident and necessary features of an evolving world, are incompatible with any form of strict determinism, whether physical or logical. He was deeply impressed by the multifariousness of nature, by the evident increase in complexity suggested by the theory of evolution, by novelty or the apparently unprecedented and unpredictable. A deterministic world, he said, could never produce such novelties or genuine surprises. Santayana, as will be emphasized presently, thought it possible to account for such phenomena in terms of the "plasticity" and the ultimate "contingency" or "chance" at the heart of existence.

And finally, it is simply unphilosophic or unscientific, Peirce claimed, to assume the truth of the deterministic thesis, as many determinists admitted they did. The claim that science is actually possible only if determinism is true, though it is still made, seemed to Peirce the very antithesis of the scientific spirit or attitude. Science, he insisted, need never postulate anything at all, much less something so contrary to what experience so plainly teaches. Law and order in nature are better regarded as in need of explanation, he suggested in accord with his second argument, than as the *sine qua non* of all scientific understanding. In other words, the causal order in nature, he thought, may very well be the product or result of evolutionary processes, rather than an aboriginal and underivative characteristic of existence. The similarity of Santayana's conviction is interesting, although there is no evidence he knew Peirce's argument and his thoroughgoing materialism made fundamental differences quite inevitable. The similarity is however limited largely to the fact that Santayana thought of law as essentially the outcome of "the concrete strains and stresses" due to particular arrangements and processes in the flux of matter.[6] There is, then, he thought, no universal law in terms of which events may be explained; yet there is also no genuine chance or self-determination in any element of existence.

In contrast to Peirce, William James was convinced that determinism must be denied, not primarily because of metaphysical or logical reasons but because moral experience, he thought, is completely unintelligible in terms of it. A deterministic world, he argued, would leave no room for alternatives and thus no room for guilt and regret; all the sorrows and evils of both the past and the future are equally inevitable and fruitless if determinism is true. But the very essence of the moral claim—its undeniable meaning—according to James, is that the conditions of existence do not demand or require the immoral act. Morality is possible or meaningful, he insisted, only if in the case of murder, for example, another world not including the murder is actually possible right up to the moment when the murderer makes his choice and performs his deed.[7]

Thus both Peirce and James emphasized the role of "chance" in natural events and processes. But neither thought of chance as a positive cause. Peirce said that he used the concept "chiefly to make room for a principle of generalization, or tendency to form habits, which . . . has produced all regularities."[8] And for James the concept of chance was essentially a mode of articulating the principle of pluralism or the ultimate reality of individuals. In a world in which certain elements are truly independent, he suggested, or where each has "something of its own," there must be chance or the genuine possibility that events might have happened differently. Such independence of things from each other, James claimed, is required in order to make intelligible such diverse but related notions as will, freedom, morality, and purpose. Santayana, as already noted, also appealed to "chance." But the meaning he attached to the term was significantly different from its meaning in Peirce and James. "Accidents," he could say, "have discoverable causes"[9] because "chance" as he conceived it was simply the absence of complete regularity or the lack of any ultimate reason for things being as they are. To Santayana chance did not imply in the least that any particular event or outcome might have been different.

But before looking more closely at Santayana's treatment of determinism and teleology, it will prove helpful to look briefly at the "consummation" of the pragmatic view in the philosophy of John Dewey, since it was this version that Santayana in fact criticized most directly. Dewey combined in his own way certain elements from the pragmatism of both Peirce and James. Like James he was profoundly concerned with the moral implications of "the-determinism-versus-freedom-and-purpose" argument. But unlike James, and closer to Peirce, he saw freedom as a function of the entire situation, rather than primarily an attribute of individuals. Man cannot be free, he was convinced, in a completely deterministic world. "Freedom is the power to act in accordance with choice"[10] but choice and power depend significantly on the total context of thought and action and not simply on the individual. "Freedom is a growth; an attainment, not an original possession, and it is attained by idealization of institutions and law and the active participation of individuals in their loyal maintainence. . . ."[11] The reference here is of course clearly to social and political freedom and the implications for law, education, religion, etc. But there can be no doubt that Dewey thought that such individual action, choice, growth, and participation are possible only because nature or existence has one character rather than another. Both freedom and the most serious threats to freedom, he said, are indeed due alike "to one outstanding fact: the evidence that the world of empirical things includes the uncertain, unpredictable, uncontrollable, and hazardous."[12] Or perhaps more to the point, he added a few pages later, "We live in a world which is an impressive and irresistible mixture of sufficiencies, tight completenesses, order, recurrences which make possible prediction and control, and singularities, ambiguities, uncertain possibilities, processes going on to consequences as yet indeterminate. They are mixed not mechanically but vitally like the wheat and tares of the parable."[13] In such a world independence and choice are clearly possible; but so are habits, dependence, and regularity. Consequently "choice is not arbitrary, not in a universe like this one, a world which is not finished and which has not consistently made up its mind where it is going and what it is going to do."[14] Human purpose and failure are significantly possible, and possible in the strictest sense of the terms, because man himself can *choose* one outcome rather than another for indeterminate processes. But his choice is by no means absolute and "every crisis, whether of the individual or the community," he observed, "reminds man of the precarious and partial nature of the control he exercises."[15]

Santayana, in a review of the book in which most of these claims were presented, labeled Dewey's naturalistic metaphysics "halfhearted and short-winded" and emphasized that "natural events" were wrongly "conceived to be compounded of such qualities as appear to human observers." "Nature is accordingly simply experience deployed, thoroughly specious and pictorial. . . . Experience is deputed to include everything to which experience might testify: it is the locus of public facts. It is therefore identical with nature, to the extent and in the aspects in which nature is disclosed to man."[16] He insisted that Dewey's belief that the future may be at least partially determined by cultivating today the qualities desired in the future is "the most terrible illusion, for it supposes that the eventual . . . is controllable by the immediate, as by wishes, omens, or high thoughts; in other words, that the essences given in the immediate exist, generate their own presence, and may persist and rearrange themselves and so generate the future. But this is sheer superstition and trust in magic."[17] This is almost certainly an exaggerated and unjustified account and critique of themes that are of course suggested by Dewey; it indicates nonetheless certain important features of Santayana's philosophy better perhaps than some of his more moderate and direct statements of it do. His conviction of complete dependence and that existence is basically an external material permanency, completely unknown and unresponsive to human demands, made Dewey's claim that ideas are instruments for knowing nature and solving problems seem horribly anthropomorphic and romantic.

One important point that should be emphasized here is that all the pragmatists may be called, more or less appropriately, *teleologists*. At least each insisted in his own way that purpose or goals, if only the purposes and goals of man, are significant factors in the outcome of natural processes. The pragmatists were perhaps all equally dubious in regard to the rational and theological (or cosmic) forms of teleology that described existence as a coherent whole, the best of all possible worlds where accidents and evils are only illusory aspects of man's limited and temporal life. But though nature has, according to the pragmatists, perhaps no one overriding purpose, purposes, they thought, play nonetheless genuine and undeniable roles in it.

Equally relevant here is the fact that the pragmatists, in accord with the long tradition of science and philosophy, constructed their views on the assumption that existence must be somehow, if not ultimately and completely, intelligible. Both the defenders and the critics of determinism, for example, justified their respective views in part by the claim that existence, at least in one aspect or another, is not otherwise intelligible. The determinists began by assuming, as Chauncey Wright in effect admitted, that to understand is to know a law and the particular facts that together "explain"—or render intelligible or inevitable—a particular event or series of events. Peirce, as already noted, objected to this view precisely because it seemed to make such crucial elements of existence as mind, growth, and novelty quite unintelligible or inexplicable. And James and Dewey insisted that determinism could not be regarded as true because it is incompatible with the apparent meaning of such important matters as moral experience and the goals of social organization and improvement.

To the bewilderment and irritation of those who so understood the philosophic enterprise, Santayana claimed in effect that such intelligibility as is usually assumed or demanded is neither possible nor necessary. Indeed, he professed to care very "little for 'explanations' (not often finding that they explain anything or make things clearer)" and so preferred "interpretations" that "express the tastes of the mind and its affections."[18] As early as his doctoral dissertation on the philosophy of Lotze, he suggested that the regularity associated with natural law does not render existence intelligible. "The mere regularity of events," he wrote, "the mere fact that things instead of happening only once happen again and again in the same ways, does not explain the world or make it rational."[19] This theme, which he confessed was due to the influence of James, was to recur again and again. He acknowledged that "when reason awakes in a man it asks for reasons for everything. Yet this demand," he added, "is unreasonable: there cannot be a reason for everything."[20] Thus beginning with the assumption that existence as such is inexplicable and that both science and philosophy must be possible, if they are possible at all, in something less than a wholly rational or intelligible world, Santayana was not tempted to appeal to either determinism or indeterminism, to chance or teleology, as a way of securing the rationality of any aspect of existence. The causal order and the resulting categories of explanation, basic though they are existentially, are not philosophically important, he suggested, because they are neither knowable nor subject to evaluation; thus they make no difference to the qualities of the spiritual or intellectual life. "For spirit is addressed to qualitative being, such as pure attention would discover in every image of sense, in every feeling, in every event: the eternal essence of that image, of that feeling, of that event. This is what poetry, painting, and history arrest and preserve."[21] To know the immediate causes of things does not *explain* why they exist and is not necessarily a good for the spirit.

Santayana clearly denied determinism in the sense in which the scientific determinists meant it, and apparently because he was inclined to agree with the pragmatists that certain aspects of existence can be what they evidently are only if there is some *indetermination* or *chance* when these mean *irregularity*. He saw no difficulty in this view. "All events may remain contingent, all laws ideally changeable and perhaps actually plastic or only approximately applicable even when they apply."[22] But he may be nonetheless with good reason called a *nondeterministic fatalist,* since he also insisted that not individual effort, purpose, or intention but rather "Chance, matter, fate—some nonspiritual principle or other—must have determined what the spirit in me shall behold, and what it shall endure. Some internal fatality, their own brute existence and wilfulness, must be responsible for the fact that things are as they are, and not otherwise."[23] In spite of the reference here to the "determined," however, he evidently did not mean "determined" as the determinists meant it; for he denied all universal principles of causality or laws in terms of which every event could be theoretically predicted or understood. Yet materialism, he clearly thought, implies some regularity in the sequence of events, though "matter is indeed not determined exactly to reproduce its previous forms, but tumbles forward to fresh collocations. . . . Believers in necessity have caught some kind of essence—a law or habit or rule of some kind—which they make haste to clap upon nature, as if nature had no further depth, and they had touched bottom with their proverbs."[24] Nature is contingent and inexplicable both in the sense that any backward survey in search of ultimate causes must stop, not with law, but with "some arbitrary state of things,"[25] and in the sense that chance or chaos is no less imaginable than law or order as the original state of things. Indeed he ventured the guess that "Chaos is perhaps at the bottom of everything: which would explain why perfect order is so rare and precarious." But although *chance* thus became the only explanation of certain events, chance never meant, as it did for James, independence or self-determination, but only contingency at the basis and plasticity in the character of existence. So law, he suggested with Peirce and Dewey, is something "achieved" rather than given, though his meaning is of course by no means the same as theirs. The chief difference perhaps is that for Peirce and Dewey law comes about as the fulfillment of purpose or direction in the affairs of man or nature and represents the achievement of *meaningful* processes and relations. But for Santayana law simply happens. "In a contingent world necessity is a conspiracy of accidents."[26] Law is then essentially only the line of least resistance in the flux of matter, a spontaneous regularity that may be described by a generalization subject even to radical exceptions.

So one result of this unusual and curious view of determinism and contingency is that Santayana could say with the scientific determinists that "Accidents have discoverable causes"[27] and "are accidents only to ignorance" or that "in reality all physical events flow out of one another by a continuous intertwined derivation." But he could also add, as few if any scientific determinists would, that "What we call the laws of nature are hasty generalisations; and even if some of them actually prevailed without exception or alloy, the fact that these laws and not others (or none) were found to be dominant would itself be groundless; so that nothing could at bottom be more arbitrary than what always happens, or more fatal than what happens but once or by absolute chance."[28] Nature, he thought, is obviously turbid, chaotic, and lawless in many respects; yet there are also "clear stretches" and "traceable currents." Wisdom will not attempt to predict and much less to control the future.

Contrary to James and Dewey, Santayana saw no relation at all between indeterminism and moral responsibility; morality, as he understood it, does not depend in the least on the assumption that the individual person may determine in some respects the outcome of precarious and otherwise unpredictable situations. Indeed he was by no means tempted to believe that man or man's will is in any degree free or self-determined. "Surely if anything ever had a cause and was evidently secondary," he wrote, "it is human will and fancy; to take them for absolute things, or original powers, would be to allow theoretical sophistries to blind us to the plainest facts." And among the plainest facts, he suggested, are these: "If I want water, it is because my throat is parched; if I dream of love, it is because sex is ripening within me. Nature has fixed the character, and circumstances have fixed the occasion, for this ferment of desire and conception." And of course from such premises it follows inevitably that "Conscious will is a symptom, not a cause; its roots as well as its consequences are invisible to it, material and often incongruous and astonishing."[29] He argued accordingly that medicine and psychology now confirm "that virtues and vices are equally phases of a controllable physical life: a fact which takes nothing away from their beauty or horror. They are the moral qualities of a natural being."[30] Consequently moral freedom, he believed, has nothing to do with choice. "We are morally free when the spirit in us sees and intends what we do physically or assents to it while being done; but spiritually we are no less implicated in actions or thoughts which we heartily approve ideally than in those which we perform or utter materially."[31] The belief that indeterminism is required for morality, he argued, is due simply to the confused notion that laws or ideas are powers that cause or create the realities or actions which in fact they only describe. But the good remains good and evil is no less evil, he was convinced, no matter what the cause involved. And responsibility for an action, he said, implies only that "it was thoroughly explicable, and caused by the man's Will, by the deepest and most ancient currents of his being; so that his action is a perfect mirror and revelation of himself—a revelation of himself perhaps appalling to his own conscience."[32]

Obviously, however, such an account of moral freedom and responsibility cannot acknowledge, as the pragmatist emphasis on indeterminism can, the enormous, and apparently incommensurable, difference between *wanting* a drink of water (which certainly comes unsummoned) and the *action* that evidently depends at least in part on *choosing* to drink or not to drink. It may of course be the case that *choosing* depends ultimately as much on material causes beyond the control of the individual as does *desiring*. Phenomenologically nonetheless—or insofar as consciousness grasps, as Santayana himself claimed, appearances only—there is an incommensurable and important difference between *feeling the desire* for a drink of water and *choosing to act* on that desire, particularly when a moral question or conflict is also involved. And to assert that there is no difference is not only to claim that experience is completely misleading but also to deny that man can learn at all from past experience or calculate the implications of present circumstances for the future and modify his own actions accordingly.

This account is of course altogether consistent with the denial of teleological elements in moral judgments. And one of Santayana's firmest convictions was that teleology or final causes may be distinguished only in "moral retrospect" as forms of poetic and religious imagination or "as moral perspectives superposed on natural causation."[33] Considered philosophically, he said, teleology, like explanation in terms of habit or law, is only a form of "mock explanation."[34] Nature aims at nothing; human action is never caused or explained by its purpose, intention, or fruition. Instead a "previous blind disposition" is realized in a complex of actions accompanied by a sense of the presence and fulfillment of purpose. The same inscrutable forces that cause the desire for water also cause the sense of purpose and choice involved in the process of satisfying thirst. But any notion that such purpose, aim, or intention is ever part of the conditions necessary to bring such desire to fruition is simply "mythical and created by a sort of literary illusion."[35] This means apparently that although an individual could not describe the total character and quality of his experience, of his ideas and feelings, without including a description of the purposes that may precede or accompany his activities, such purposes in no sense actually cause or sustain the activities of the individual. "Ideas at best can be only the formal or final causes of their exemplification: they are not forces at all, but qualities and harmonies resulting from the concourse of material facts: and to say that the form or function of anything 'makes' it what it is, is a mere play on the ambiguity of words and a solemn mystification."[36] Thus the claim that final causes do "exist in the conduct of human beings,"[37] which Santayana did make, can mean only that ideals, wishes, and purposes "are mental echoes of movements proper to bodily life. . . . The more accurately they prefigure events . . . the better they prove their own fidelity to the ruling impulses of matter."[38]

One way to emphasize the philosophical novelty, if not the importance, of such antiteleological convictions is to point out that the good, the harmony, the lure of feeling, or the longing for perfection, or concepts that have played such important and apparently necessary roles in the thought of such philosophers as Plato, Aristotle, Peirce, Whitehead, and Bergson, had no place at all in Santayana's thoroughgoing materialism. As opposed to Aristotle, nothing, much less all things, aims at the good. Nature or existence as such, or an individual, never aims at or achieves anything at all because it is desirable or good. For "what arises is not the good, in any prior or absolute sense, but only the possible at that juncture: a natural growth which as it takes form becomes good in its own eyes, or in the eyes of a sympathetic poet."[39] "All the furniture of the earth and the choir of heaven," far from being created by God *for* his own glory and the benefit of man, are ultimately fortuitous collocations of atoms, accidents in which even the apparent purposes of man are better regarded as illusions than as reflections of some design or purpose in existence. The intentions of man can contribute nothing to the most magnificent results of his labor. And existence or nature is truly if not "benignly indifferent" to all the possibilities that wait in the realm of essence for the *chance* to be exemplified in the flux of matter. Although this view was clearly compatible with certain presuppositions in the physics and biology of the age, it nonetheless made much of human experience and activity altogether meaningless or unintelligible.

This chapter should then not end without an extended note on the inconsistency and ambiguity in Santayana's approach to the problems of determinism and teleology. And surely one important and relevant consideration is that he often wrote as if the claims here attributed to him were false. The very title of his first major work, *The Life of Reason or The Phases of Human Progress,* suggested that reason or intelligence, together with the freedom and purpose this normally implies, has at least some minimum and important part in the course of events, particularly in the social order, religion, art, and science. Yet even there he wrote, "Anyone who can at all catch the drift of experience—moral no less than physical—must feel that mechanism rules the whole world." And he added that "Mechanism is the dialectic of the irrational."[40] This conviction was perhaps related to an aspect of his life and work recorded much later in an autobiographical article: "I have seldom been conscious of working hard," he wrote. "Most of my writing has been an instinctive pleasure, a playful impulse, as in running down a grassy slope or exploring a woodland path. The things wrote themselves; and when I dropped the pen, and rose from my writing table, I seemed to awake from a trance and to be myself again."[41] This is of course quite consistent with the profound sense of dependence already noted; and surely the feeling that the most serious work is achieved automatically would encourage the conclusion that the creative forces are completely below the surface, that aims and efforts are also the results of subterranean processes and can be only poetically or mythically regarded as in any measure the outcome of conscious purpose or intention. And no doubt automatic processes do account for much that has all the appearances of careful planning and purposive effort.

The philosophically notable element in this, however, is that Santayana apparently never seriously examined the logical difficulties involved in claiming that all ideas are indifferently the results of automatic physical processes. He was evidently unaware of the paradoxical nature of the claim that all ideas—which must of course include this one—are due exclusively to the dark depths and automatic processes in matter, and never to the mind's own discovery that certain ideas are the logical consequences of others. But it is very odd, to say the least, that there should be ideas about the origin of ideas, and quite impossible to know whether such ideas are true, if this account of the causal order is correct. And to enter a disclaimer, as Santayana occasionally did, to the effect that what one has written neither is nor aspires to be true, while perhaps admirable in its modesty, does not avoid in the least the logical difficulties involved in denying that existence has the character one has already attributed to it. To admit that purpose, freedom, and effort are elements of experience but yet deny that they have any existential significance seems indeed the very antithesis of an undogmatic scepticism in search of the minimum claims on which a life of reason (or a spiritual life) may be based. Consequently the temptation is to say of Santayana, as he said of the Stoic, Marcus Aurelius, that he seems to be two: the one modestly insisting that all judgments, including his own, are symbolic and tentative, partial and groping; and the other quite confident that this view and the materialism by which it is presumably both generated and justified reflect the actual and inevitable condition of all human existence and knowledge. For surely one cannot claim with any assurance that man's experience and account of things are merely symbolic and illusory without assuming that he has himself somehow and in some measure escaped the limits imposed by his own instruments and conditions. And a philosophy based completely on materialistic determinism can apparently provide no way by which the validity of ideas can be tested, and so only increases paradoxes as it intensifies its search for the truth.

Chapter 7

GOD, RELIGION, AND POETRY

"Believe? . . . It is too gross
And palpable a fiction, fit for those
Who dream awake."

Lucifer, Act IV

Evidently George Santayana was at least sometimes tempted to think of himself as truly religious, particularly in contrast to both those who presumably regarded religious ideas and activities superstitiously and those who completely denied the meaning and value of all religious symbols. Yet he also noted on occasion that a religion must invariably appeal to a faith that he could not share, or that religion can be distinguished from poetry only insofar as it involves *faith* in the *literal* as opposed to the *symbolic* truth of its claims. He was certainly convinced that the beliefs generally called "religious" are for the most part superstitions if taken literally, though he also clearly believed that religion, even when it is superstitious, can be in some respects an embodiment of reason. For "the roots of reason and superstition are intertwined in the mind," he said, "and society has always expressed and cultivated them together."[1] But unlike other philosophers of the time who took religion seriously, he had no interest at all in proving the existence of God or the immortality of the soul. Indeed, in the traditional meanings of the terms, he was convinced that God does not exist and that nothing is immortal. To be truly religious, as distinguished from being superstitious, is then to recognize that "Religion is an interpretation of the world, honestly made, and made in view of man's happiness and its empirical conditions"[2] or that religious claims are poetic, symbolic, or ideal and never literal or factual. If it is impious and irreligious to deny or despise the very traditions that are the sources of one's own existence, he suggested, it is superstition to suppose that a religious account of the origin and destiny of man can ever be more than myth or fable.

But although he denied the existence of God, Santayana's respect for the moral importance and meaning of the theism of the Judeo-Christian tradition was no doubt sincere if not really profound. Man's impotence, fear, and need, his utter dependence on inscrutable powers that constantly threaten to forsake him "furnish the proof of God's existence . . . as mankind originally perceived it."[3] So although God cannot be said to exist, "Nothing could be clearer than the grounds on which pious men in the beginning recognize divine agencies."

> We see, they say, the hand of God in our lives. He has saved us from dangers, he has comforted us in sorrow. He has blessed us with the treasures of life, of intelligence, of affection. He has set around us a beautiful world, and one still more beautiful within us. . . . In other words, pious men discern God in the excellence of things. . . . The pleasantness of life, the preciousness of human possessions, the beauty and promise of the world, are proofs of God's power; so is the stilling of tempests and the forgiveness of sin. . . . God is the ideal, and what manifests the ideal manifests God. The proof and measure of rationality in the world, and of God's power over it, is the extent of human satisfactions.[4]

Existence thus generates and sustains ideas of God in the minds of men. And this, he thought, is what is religiously important. "Proofs of the existence of God are therefore not needed, since his existence is in one sense obvious and in another of no religious interest." There is no need of proof, he suggested, simply because God *is* an ideal present to the mind of man, and "the ideal is a term of moral experience." And proof of God's existence is of no religious interest or importance because the significance of moral ideals, he insisted, is not changed by the fact that they may originate in "some physical or dynamic absolute . . . scientifically discoverable in the dark entrails of nature or of mind."[5] In other words, religion as the poetic or symbolic expression of ideals is not morally impoverished by the fact that the ideals expressed do not exist.

Consequently Saint Augustine's conception of God, except for the notion that God is "the creator of all essence and existence," is, Santayana claimed, admirable and essentially sound. "God, to him, was simply the ideal eternal object of human thought and love. . . . He was never tired of telling us that God is not true but the truth (i.e., the ideal object of thought in any sphere), not good but the good (i.e., the ideal object of will in all its rational manifestations)." Thus morally considered, for Augustine, "God signified the comprehensive ideal of all the perfections which the human spirit could behold in itself or in its objects."[6] This interpretation of Augustine may of course be seriously biased or limited. But the important point here is that according to Santayana God is an ideal and only an ideal. He does not exist but is better than anything that does exist; for he is a product of imagination or idealization, the perfection that existence everywhere suggests but nowhere attains. God's *reality* (a term that he would consent to use without existential implications) is not different from the reality of perfect circles and golden mountains. The conception implies existence in neither case.

God then must not be identified with the whole of nature or the order of nature any more than a perfect circle is to be identified with the sum of imperfect circles. "Nature neither is nor can be man's ideal. The substitution of nature for the traditional and ideal object of religion involves giving nature moral authority over man."[7] And since nothing that exists is more or less natural than anything else, to imitate nature is to abandon everything humane. Consequently, although God does not exist and the very idea of God is wholly poetic or mythical, the concept is nonetheless highly relevant to man's moral and spiritual life. Indeed, "the idea of God as Lord and Lawgiver represents dramatically the contact of spirit with all external powers. Respect for these powers is wisdom." He accordingly suggested that religion might be defined in part as "the recognition of the Powers on which our destiny truly depends, and the art of propitiating those Powers and of living, as far as the power in us avails, in devout harmony with them."[8] But apparently much more important for the highest religions than the recognition of the Powers is "the idea of God as spirit, loving the spirit in us and realising in himself all that spirit in us looks to as its supreme good. . . ." For this idea "is evidently prophetic; that is, it sees in a vision as an accomplished fact, though hidden from vulgar apprehension, a secret ideal of the heart, and helps to render that ideal clearer and more communicable."[9] Or with a slightly different emphasis, in the pursuit of truth, he said, God may be regarded as "a poetic symbol for the maternal tenderness and the paternal strictness of this wonderful world."[10]

Why, if the idea of God seemed so clearly relevant to the moral and spiritual life, did Santayana deny his existence? There is no obvious answer to this question. In part, however, his atheism (if such a nonmilitant, reverent, and poetic denial of God's existence must bear the arrogant implications of this label) was simply a concomitant of his materialism and of the conviction that all religious symbols must accordingly be ideal interpretations of experience and not descriptions of existing things. This view, as indicated already in the account of his life, seems not to have been the result of any personal or religious crisis or the culmination of philosophical argument. He implied that he came to the position gradually; and it might have been in part an interpretation of experience suggested by both current scientific theories and the diversity of religious beliefs and practices. He knew in detail the histories of various religions and suggested that only when they are dead do "they manifest their virtues to the unbeliever. He sees that they are expressions of human genius; that however false to their subject-matter they may be, like the conventions of art they are true to the eye and to the spirit that fashioned them." But equally important, "The sting is gone out of their errors . . . and they have acquired a beauty invisible to the eye of their authors, because of the very refraction which the truth suffered in that vital medium."[11]

In any case there is in all of Santayana's writings only one serious and extended discussion of the arguments for the existence of God—and this seeks only to show that the ontological argument for God's existence does not succeed. Furthermore, his basic concern even in this discussion was not to criticize or question religious claims as such but rather to deny that there are any necessary truths. He attached little or no religious significance to the fact that, in his opinion, the ontological argument failed to demonstrate the existence of God. Yet it seems relevant to note the main features of his rebuttal. Following St. Anselm's version, he noted that the ontological argument claims —on the assumption that a being that lacks no perfection cannot lack existence—that the most real of beings *(ens realissimum)* must exist necessarily; "for evidently if it did not exist, far from being most real, it would not be real at all." However, Santayana did not follow Immanuel Kant's precedent and claim that this argument is fallacious simply because *existence,* unlike *goodness, omniscience,* etc., is not a predicate required to complete the *conception* of God's perfection. Instead, he insisted that the argument could be cogent only if it were already granted that power is "the first mark of reality and value." But the argument would then be only an extended tautology since "power is only another name for the difference which the existence of one thing makes in the existence of another."[12] But he also claimed that, as it stands, the argument might be construed to prove the nonexistence rather than the existence of God—if, following the Hindus, the greater value is attached to nonexistence and reality is identified with Pure Being. But the argument, he insisted, is "fallacious and even ridiculous if by 'necessary existence' we understand a necessity attaching to events or to facts, that is to contingencies."[13] If a proposition is necessarily true, he concluded, the terms must be only essences defining the idea in question. Therefore, if the term "God" means "a psychological moral being energizing in space and time, then his existence can be proved only by the evidence of these natural manifestations, not by dialectical reasoning upon the meanings of terms."[14]

Accordingly, at the end of *The Realm of Spirit,* he noted again that "By definition there is an *ens realissimum*" but insisted that this *most real of beings* is simply a name for "all the radical, pervasive, and terrible influences to which the spirit is subject." So the question, Does God exist? is only verbal, he added, and the genuine question is "whether the reality signified by the notion of God, if we understood that reality better, could still bear the name of God, or had better be designated by some other word." He then reaffirmed that his own philosophy, since it "puts all substance and power into the realm of matter," is consequently atheistic.[15]

Santayana's easy dismissal of the ontological argument is of course possible only by virtue of his radical distinction between essence and existence. The cosmological argument, appealing to the need and evidence for divine power and intelligence in the order of nature, obviously seemed to him, as parts of the quotations above indicate, much more important and persuasive than merely rational arguments. In his dissertation on Lotze he in fact argued that the cosmological argument, insisting on a will as the necessary first cause of order in the universe, is required because ordinary causal or mechanistic explanation "really fails to explain anything."[16] In his mature philosophy, however, there is neither defense nor criticism of the cosmological argument except for one brief and indirect mention in *Scepticism and Animal Faith* where he suggested that "If the cosmos were a single animal, as the ancients supposed, and had an aim and a life which, like human life, could be fulfilled in the contemplation of certain essences, then a life like that of Aristotle's God would be involved in the perfection of nature, if this perfection was ever attained."[17] At least partly because he regarded theology, not as a genuine element of religion, but as metaphysical inquiry, and thought his own materialism was antimetaphysical, he could not take seriously theological argument of any kind.

Religion, Santayana thought, is primarily a product not of reason but of imagination and is more closely related to poetry and the other arts than to philosophic and scientific enterprises—though the mistake should not be made of supposing that he thought either philosophy or science can provide a literal or completely accurate description of existence. But he insisted nonetheless that science, if not philosophy, is based on actual practice and perception, and that on this level "close scrutiny and the principle of parsimony" are sufficient to distinguish "fable from knowledge."[18] In other words, "The terms of astronomy are essences no less human and visionary than those of mythology; but they are the fruit of a better focused, more chastened, and more prolonged attention turned upon what actually occurs; that is, they are kept closer to animal faith, and freer from pictorial elements and the infusion of reverie."[19] But religions are wholly imaginative interpretations of experience and should not be considered knowledge of existence at all in the same sense that science is, though they may express, in their own way and better than the symbols of philosophy and the sciences, certain aspects of the moral and spiritual life of man. Religion provides, however, no information at all about worlds beyond the natural world or a life after death. Any reliable knowledge about such matters, he was obviously convinced, must come through the same sort of experience as that on which science is based. Religion, although it may claim to reveal the most important truths, can in fact express only ideals, attitudes, obligations, and goals, or cultivate piety, charity, and spirituality or aspiration in the life of man. And there is no truth but only convention and fable in such matters. Consequently "religious belief is terribly precarious, partly because it is arbitrary, so that in the next tribe or in the next century it will wear quite a different form; and partly because, when genuine, it is spontaneous and continually remodelled, like poetry, in the heart that gives it birth." And simply because religion is so "fantastic and insecure," it is "jealously defended" and thus becomes the "outer ring . . . of the fortifications of prejudice."[20]

But although religion is fantastic, mythical, and so never literally true, it may be, Santayana thought, nonetheless profoundly meaningful. And the great difference in this respect between his view and that of the contemporary positivists and empiricists, who have dismissed all religious language as cognitively meaningless, should be carefully noted. He of course agreed with the positivists and empiricists—though his reasons are significantly different—that serious concern on the part of philosophers about the *truth* of religion is grossly misplaced, since truth in religion is irrelevant, particularly if one means by "truth" only the claims that can be verified by sensory experience. But this, he obviously thought, does not imply that religion has no intellectual content or is completely irrelevant to "the life of reason." "Religion pursues rationality through imagination. . . . Thus religion has the same original relation to life that poetry has."[21] And the "poet, before science exists, is . . . the man of truest and most adequate vision. His persuasion that he knows the heart and soul of things is no fancy reached by artificial inference or analogy but is a direct report of his own experience and honest contemplation."[22] Indeed, he claimed, "the poetic value of religion" is "initially . . . greater than that of poetry itself, because religion deals with higher and more practical themes, with sides of life which are in greater need of some imaginative touch and ideal interpretation. . . ." And in an even more direct statement of its function, religion is said to be "an imaginative achievement, a symbolic representation of moral reality which may have a most important function in vitalising the mind and in transmitting, by way of parables, the lessons of experience."[23] Thus contrary to the positivistic accounts of religion, Santayana insisted that the value and meaning of the moral and spiritual life are best expressed in religious symbols. Precisely because religion is so profoundly meaningful, it is subject to abuse and may become a radical and continuous deception that "can work indefinite harm in the world and in the conscience."[24] But even an absurd religion may "furnish a happy interlude in a drab life, a peep-hole into fairyland, a little secret unsuspected by the world, to keep up . . . self-respect, and cast a ray of supernatural hope. . . ."[25] The positivist might of course be tempted to claim that in denying the literal truth of religion Santayana in effect agreed with him that religion has only "emotive meaning"—a meaning entirely different from the intellectual content of science. But this approach would of course ignore the very important fact that Santayana also denied that science can be "literally" true. Furthermore, he was clearly convinced that religion may have an intellectual content not different so much in degree as in kind from the intellectual content of science and philosophy. When he said that religion is not true he meant essentially only that there are no existing entities corresponding to its most important symbols. But this, he thought, does not prevent religion from making essentially true claims about the character and value of human existence.

Related to the positivist view is the more frequent claim that the value of religion in Santayana's account of it is wholly moral. And in the broadest sense of the term this is no doubt true. Indeed he was himself frequently inclined simply to contrast "the moral" with "the factual"; but surely to the extent that "the moral" refers only to right conduct or the ethics of action, the value of religion as he understood it includes much more than moral values. Among the most important of the extra-moral values of religion is its poetic or aesthetic quality. Religious mythologies, he said, involve "wonderful creations which have a poetic value of their own. . . ."[26] And pushing the same idea further, he added that religious images, like the images of art, "have other properties and other uses for the spirit besides their value as signals relevant to action. They have intrinsic form; and precisely because they are in a manner illusions, they are originals; ideal objects interesting in themselves."[27] In the narrow sense of the term it may in fact be claimed that he thought the moral function of religion is quite secondary. "Indeed, the most characteristic function of religion would seem to lie in lifting the soul out of its earthly environment altogether and bringing it into an imagined commerce with supernatural things.[28] (The "supernatural" means here of course only that which is better than —and not that which exists beyond—nature.) The religious imagination accomplishes its task by providing "those large ideas tinctured with passion, those supersensible forms shrouded in awe, in which alone a mind of great sweep and vitality can find its congenial objects."[29] Religion is primarily a perspective; and in its perspective tragedy becomes poetry; "the hopes and sorrows of the world become arguments for religion. Evils remain as bad as ever for the natural man; but for the spirit in him they are transformed; what was a predicament becomes a vista, what was a puzzle becomes a truth."[30] Thus religion, like all the major arts, extends the range of the spirit and enables man to grow "larger by thinking himself so large. . . ."[31] And surely such functions must be called *ontological* as well as *moral*, since they obviously contribute as much (even in Santayana's own view) to man's being as to his action.

Indeed in his final major work, *Dominations and Powers,* Santayana made clearer perhaps than he ever had before that he regarded "the principle of rational morality" as "utterly independent of each and all religion, and rather inimical to any special gospel." For rational morality, he thought, is bound to take appropriate account of all the interests and needs of life while any particular religion "attributes a unique and final authority to one type of value and to one passionate interest."[32] A religion includes special moral principles and its own sanctions, both generated and supported by its own imaginative view of existence. So from the point of view of a rational morality, he argued, religion loads the dice and is "a moral heresy"; therefore the decline of religion, "far from undermining the general principle of morality, sets that principle free and permits human morality to become rational and normal."[33] Presumably then a life could be perfectly rational and moral without any religion at all—even more rational and moral indeed without religion than with it. Yet religion, he thought, is nonetheless a great benefit for the spirit, an intrinsic good that men would not otherwise possess. And if the religions must be sometimes severely censured or condemned, this only justifies another and not incompatible judgment: "The necessity of rejecting and destroying some things that are beautiful is the deepest curse of existence."[34]

Santayana's treatment of religion was surely one of the most distinctive features of his thought. And the difference between his views and the views of the pragmatists on this topic is immense and indicative of other important differences in their respective philosophical perspectives. Oddly enough the pragmatist whose approach to religion was most orthodox, C. S. Peirce, apparently shared both the greatest similarity and the greatest difference with Santayana in this respect—though the similarity even in this case is largely superficial and not extensive. Perhaps it is simply Peirce's great respect for tradition and orthodoxy in religion that accounts for the impression that his view of religion is closer than that of James or Dewey to Santayana's treatment. For in spite of the fact that Santayana's religious views have been most severely criticized by Catholic theologians, there is in his thought a profound sympathy for the spirit and symbolism, if not for the word and literal truth, of the Christian tradition, particularly as represented by Catholicism—a sympathy that is largely if not completely lacking in most other contemporary secular philosophers.

Peirce, who apparently had an almost instinctive faith in the relevance of the religious or theological approach to certain problems of existence, shared with Santayana at least the conviction that religious belief is really more a matter of instinct and experience than of argument. He thought that the best evidence for the existence of God occurs in what he called "Musement"—which, as he described it, was surely close to the contemplative activity of the spirit as Santayana conceived it. "Musement," said Peirce, is "Pure Play" with no rules. "It bloweth where it listeth. It has no purpose, unless recreation." But such aimless activity suggests "God's reality" because the mind of man responds to this "attractive fancy" "for its beauty, for its supplying an ideal of life, and for its thoroughly satisfactory explanation of his threefold environment."[35] Santayana of course, though he agreed that religion involves great beauty and ideals, could not conceive of a "thoroughly satisfactory explanation" of any sort, much less that a theological or religious account could explain existence in its various forms. But Peirce apparently never doubted seriously the profound metaphysical or moral significance of religion. He certainly would never have settled for Santayana's account of the symbolic character of religious beliefs, though he would no doubt have agreed that they ought not be taken as literally as is often the case.

William James's religious experience and concern were evidently more intense, and closer to the heart of his philosophy, than that of either Peirce or Santayana. Where Peirce had regarded religion as essentially a way of life, perhaps illuminated and justified by the "Musement" that suggests the reality of God, and Santayana thought religion only a symbolic expression of moral predicaments and congenial ideals, James considered religion to be primarily the most serious hypothesis possible about the nature of existence and the ultimate destiny of man. The religious hypothesis declares, he said, "that the so-called order of nature, which constitutes this world's experience, is only one portion of the total universe, and that there stretches beyond this visible world an unseen world of which we now know nothing positive, but in relation to which the true significance of our present mundane life consists."[36] But religion also insists, he claimed, that the best things are eternal and that men are better off for believing this now. James's view of religion was thus clearly such that Santayana's report that he called *Interpretations of Poetry and Religion* "a perfection of rottenness"[37] is altogether credible and understandable. For it was in this early book that Santayana first defined religion as "poetry become the guide of life, poetry substituted for science or supervening upon it as an approach to the highest reality."[38] He first made clear in this book his conviction that religion cannot be literally or factually true; and this no doubt seemed to James tantamount to a complete denial of the worth and seriousness of all religion.

John Dewey shared Santayana's conviction that God is not an actual being but in Dewey's own words, only the name for "the ideal ends that one . . . acknowledges as having authority over his volition and emotion" or "a unification of ideal values that is essentially imaginative in origin when the imagination supervenes in conduct."[39] Yet Dewey was never quite as clear as Santayana was about the total irrelevance of God so-conceived to the course and character of actual events—not being as rashly confident that matter is omnificent or the doer of all that is done; thus he was neither as frankly nor as obviously atheistic as Santayana. Yet he apparently had little if any of Santayana's sensitivity to the beauty and meaning of religious symbols and institutions and so did not share in the least his estimate of their intrinsic value. Therefore he could not share the conviction that religious rituals and ideas are in themselves important expressions of man's spirit. To be significant, Dewey thought, an idea or symbol must function instrumentally or as a means of coping with the actual problems of existence; and in this respect religious ideas and practices, he was convinced, have very often proved absolutely useless and indeed harmful. In contrast Santayana's view of religion was clearly not pragmatic; for he claimed that religion can provide only perspectives for the spirit—and the spirit is not power but only vision. Instrumentally or pragmatically regarded religion is indeed quite useless; but this condemns it only because existence, including especially the good for man and the relevance of ideas in achieving this good, has already been woefully misconceived. A philosophy of resignation, contemplative and aesthetic, can find little to approve in the vigorous pragmatic activist who holds man himself responsible, at least in certain important respects, for his own condition and activities. The complete dependence of man, whether on God or matter, justifies equally every form of indifference and every instance of madness.

There is obviously much to question and doubt in Santayana's approach to religion, particularly if one finds it more difficult than he did to distinguish radically between meaning and existence, essence and fact, ideas and things, or if one is accustomed to thinking that the religions may, in one way or another, embody significant metaphysical or "literal" as well as moral and symbolic truths, or even if one believes as Dewey did that the religions absorb or frustrate energies that might be otherwise and more beneficently employed. But more relevant here than any account of the changes that these different approaches would demand are two quite evident and serious paradoxes that pervade his writings on religion.

Perhaps the most obvious paradox is that he insisted, on the one hand, that religion is not literally true but only symbolic of moral goods and ideal perfections, or in other words that religion, truly understood, may supervene on or transcend but cannot intervene in or modify a life; yet, on the other hand, he also claimed that in order to be religious it is necessary to believe that religious symbols are literally true. Stated bluntly, the paradox is that religion, or an immediate acquaintance with religious values, is actually impossible except for those who take a false and superstitious view of religious symbols. Apparently this paradox was already present in—though perhaps mitigated in some measure by—the early definition of religion as "poetry become the guide of life." But in an essay reportedly written about the same time as *Interpretations of Poetry and Religion,* though not published until after his death, he claimed that "in the mouth of Jesus, the kingdom of heaven is a moral symbol"[40] and that "only one who sees things as they are can have a pure religion."[41] But the paradox was compounded and became more obvious in later works. In *Reason in Society* he wrote that "Religion, when pure, contemplates some pertinent ideal of intelligence and goodness"[42] and in *Reason in Religion* he suggested that rational religion "should pass into . . . contemplation, ideality, poetry, in the sense in which poetry includes all imaginative life."[43] Similarly in *The Realm of Spirit* he claimed that "the only perfectly rational form of life for a spirit that has attained self-knowledge is the life of prayer"[44] and that "rational prayer is not a means but an end."[45] And clearly he recognized prayer as a basic and significant part of the religious life. Yet in *Winds of Doctrine* (written between *The Life of Reason* and *Realms of Being),* although he claimed that Christianity is a "moral fable,"[46] he also insisted that "it is not those who accept the deluge, the resurrection, and the sacraments only as symbols that are the vital party, but those who accept them literally; for only these have anything to say to the poor, or to the rich, that can refresh them. In a frank supernaturalism . . . lies the sole hope of the church."[47] Evidently the sum of this is that the highest values of religion both emphatically do and do not accrue only to those who regard moral fables and poetic symbols superstitiously or as literal truth.

The second paradox is no doubt related to the first and is perhaps ultimately deeper and more significant, though it is not altogether as obvious. On the one hand Santayana seemed clearly to share, even in an unusual degree, the sensibility that at least psychologically speaking is evidently the root of religion and normally results in the conviction that existence (or at least some part of it) may be most appropriately recognized as an object of worship. His style, his choice of themes and examples, his very assertions bear frequent witness to a "religious" dimension in his experience and intellect. Yet this same sensibility or dimension—or perhaps its frustration in the face of certain "facts" of existence—was also apparently responsible for the essentially "irreligious" conclusion that "the real is rotten" and that only the imaginary (or unreal) is truly good or worthy of reverence. This paradox might of course have been completely resolved either by dismissing religious symbols as meaningless expressions of emotion or by embracing some version of optimistic religious faith and dismissing all evil as illusory. Yet the fact that he did not choose either of these ways of dealing with religious experience and claims seems at least a sign, even in the midst of bad logic, of complete honesty that refused to compromise for the sake of happiness or consistency. Convinced that it would have been better to "have been born in nature's day/ When man was in the world a wide-eyed boy,/ And clouds of sorrow crossed his sky of joy/ To scatter dewdrops on the buds of May," he nonetheless candidly faced what seemed to him the bitter evidence that "no hope of heaven" can now "sweeten our few tears/ And hush the importunity of pain."[48] And if this is the case, he concluded, religions, no matter how beautiful and important, are not really true or indicative of the actual character of existence. For religious opinions and judgments, like all others, "arise in psyches and express the capacity and inevitableness of such opinions and judgments arising at each moment in the psyche; but the degree of their truth depends on the relation that their several deliverances have to the facts that provoke them and that they *mean* to refer to."[49] Since the facts that provoke all ideas are, he thought, ultimately material and the universe does not contain the kind of things that religious symbols apparently *mean* to refer to, religions must be regarded as simply imaginative myth and fable. Religion is a form of radical illusion if one regards it as true.

Chapter 8

ETHICS AND SOCIAL POLICY

> "But the nerve of moral judgment is preference: and preference is a feeling or an impulse to action which cannot be either false or true."
>
> *The Realm of Truth*

It has been noted already that George Santayana's philosophy assumed the truth of physical determinism and that he thought moral issues could be examined and understood on a completely deterministic basis. Indeed, in his first systematic treatment of moral problems, in *Reason in Science,* he articulated this assumption in unmistakable terms. "Why anyone values anything at all, or anything in particular," he declared, "is a question of physics." Consequently to account ultimately for the fact that a particular individual desires one thing rather than another at any given time is to "explain what sort of blood and training this man possessed, and what happened among the cells and fibres of his brain to make him reason after that fashion. The causes of morality, good or bad, are physical. . . ."[1] He reaffirmed this complete physical determinism in *Realms of Being,* indirectly if not directly, by claiming that "The root of morality is animal bias"[2] and that animal bias is completely dependent on the physical "machinery of growth, instinct, and action."[3] He also said there, it must be admitted—though no doubt more or less metaphorically—that "all morality is deeply social"[4] and that morality is the product neither of facts nor the consequences of facts but of "human terror or desire feeling its way amid those facts and those consequences."[5] But finally, in *Dominations and Powers,* he said again in unambiguous terms that it is an assumption, "or rather a tautology in naturalistic philosophy," that "causes are all physical"[6] and that "Physical necessity and fate, when not conceived superstitiously, are therefore the true and only foundation for living at ease."[7]

But of course Santayana never proposed to treat or explain moral problems in terms of their ultimate physical causes. Philosophical inquiry or dialectic, he admitted, can treat moral problems only *morally* or in terms of their *intent*. And the intent of moral choice or judgment, he thought, is to discover and defend or to realize and promote *the good* as it appears to a particular animal. Moral inquiry or ethics, which is the science of moral experience, cannot itself discover the ultimate origin or grounds of moral intent or preference. Ethics must then begin with the recognition of the fact that discriminations between good and evil pervade all experience. And simply because man is a specific kind of organism with various but definite needs—and impulses that seek to satisfy the needs—"moral judgments of some sort are inevitable in man. He cannot help having some radical preferences."[8] Preference and value, however, characterize not only such matters as taste, the actions that satisfy vital needs, and the relations of individuals to one another. "Value is the principle of perspective in science, no less than of rightness in life."[9] Or in the more poetic terms of his later work, "Reflected in the living soul, all the rays of nature instantly acquire a moral colour."[10] Intent or preference, although not its own cause, "sets up its own standard."[11] Consequently his moral philosophy is constructed in thoroughly traditional terms and for the most part ignores the presumed physical basis and cause of experience. Good and bad, right and wrong, harmony, freedom, reflection, and choice are (except for occasional disclaimers) treated as the ultimate and indispensable categories of experience and judgment.

A second important assumption of Santayana's moral and social philosophy is that although man is a social animal, he can nonetheless exist without government—even without society once he has been born and has achieved some maturity—and has a "latent impulse to isolation" or an "ideal of living alone with God, with nature, or with thought." In other words, at the very heart of man's existence, he claimed, is "a closed, private, indomitable life. Every man has a soul of his own." Therefore the individual is presumed to be "the only seat and focus of social forces. If society and government are to be justified at all, they must be justified in his eyes and by his instincts."[12] Or in more radical and emphatic terms, "Society exists by a conspiracy of psychological forces; however rigid you make its machinery, its breath of life must come from the willing connivance of a myriad fleeting, inconstant, half rational human souls."[13] The individual thus provides the presumed basis and standard of all moral judgment. And although he said that the ethics of Aristotle is essentially sound, nothing could be further from the Aristotelian assumption that the state or community is prior to the individual in the same sense that the body is prior to the hand or eye.

The intent or preference of the individual—the fact that an individual finds this or that good or bad, to be cherished or shunned—is then, Santayana claimed, the starting point in the dialectics of moral reason. And that which is found to be good is so presumably only because it satisfies the desires, interests, or needs of the individual. This good may be expressed as a personal preference, as an ideal or standard, or as a general rule to which the behavior of all the members of a group are expected to conform. But its authority is derived solely from the fact that it satisfies the needs or interests of an individual. And if an evaluation is honestly and carefully made, he insisted, there can be no serious question about its genuine authority or rightness unless it leads to conflict with other goods—the other desires and needs of the individual himself or the goods of other people who are somehow related to him. "Moral comparisons are possible only in view of each ideal, and after some ideal has been virtually set up."[14] And each individual or type of individual is of course subject to various interests, endeavors, perfections, and imperfections that may be expressed as moral ideals, standards, and dangers. But ideals, standards, and dangers are such only in relation to individuals. "The various ideals and types of perfection . . . are qualified and graded morally" according to "the endeavours and interests of living beings." Consequently the validity of a moral claim depends not on the object of judgment but on the nature of the judge. "Perfections may be differently prized, though each be as perfect as every other, because various sorts of perfect objects are not of equal consequence to a given animal nor in a given ideal."[15]

There is then, Santayana claimed, no such thing as *good* or *bad* except as one thing or another satisfies or frustrates the actual needs, interests, or desires of some living creature. The emphasis, however, is clearly on needs rather than interests or desires. For an individual might, he recognized, be interested in or desire the undesirable —the undesirable, that is, so far as his genuine and long-term needs and interests are concerned. Thus he was not at all tempted to say that there is nothing good or bad except thinking makes it so. For it is not what one *thinks* but rather what one *is* that determines the good for him. In order to know the truly good it is therefore necessary to know oneself. So the essence of his moral theory is that the actual good always depends on the nature of some individual and that each individual, although sharing certain generic qualities with mankind, has also his own character and needs that are not completely immutable or inflexible but are nonetheless specific and discoverable.

Santayana's most sustained and interesting argument for the claim that there are no goods independent of the specific interests and needs of individuals was constructed in an essay on the philosophy of Bertrand Russell and reputedly had the effect of causing a radical shift in the moral philosophy of the latter. In an essay on "The Elements of Ethics" Russell had argued that "Good and bad are qualities which belong to objects independently of our opinions, just as much as round and square do; and when two people differ as to whether a thing is good, only one of them can be right, though it may be very hard to know which is right."[16] He also maintained, due no doubt in part to the influence of G. E. Moore, that good is "a unique indefinable quality." So in effect his position as expressed in this essay was that *good,* although not definable in the way that geometrical properties are, is a quality that belongs to some things objectively or regardless of their relation to the needs and interests of living organisms.

Santayana readily agreed that *good* is indefinable, even as *green* or *right* or *left* is indefinable insofar as each is in the last analysis a unique quality or relation, an irreducible meaning or essence that must be given in intuition or simply grasped by the mind. Nonetheless any concrete realization of green, he argued, "is a quality that things acquire under certain conditions" and "everything that is to the right is not to the right on no condition, but obviously on the condition that someone is looking in a certain direction."[17] Similarly, he continued, although *the idea of the good* as apprehended by intuition is absolutely distinct from *the idea of evil,* specific or concrete goods can be such only in relation to the specific character and power of some life. In other words, morality must be based, not on the *idea* of the good, but on the direct experience and evaluation of the concrete goods that present themselves to a particular psyche. "The ultimate intuitions on which ethics rests are not debatable, for they are not opinions we hazard but preferences we feel; and it can be neither correct nor incorrect to feel them."[18] So contrary to Russell's claim, he insisted, it is altogether possible that two different individuals may be equally justified in their moral claims even though verbally their claims contradict each other completely. For there can be no good, he thought, apart from individual needs or preferences that are fulfilled; and needs and preferences are determined by the radically different structures and potentialities of living organisms. And if universal sympathy and cooperation should seem to be a legitimate or authoritative ideal for every creature, that is only because the implications have not been sufficiently considered. "The tigers cannot regard it as such, for it would suppress the tragic good called ferocity, which makes, in their eyes, the chief glory of the universe."[19] Or to deny tigers the *right* to be ferocious is to forget that the origins of preference are not themselves moral but natural. And the truth, he was convinced, is that "in the economy of nature there is no such thing as a right."[20]

Indeed Santayana distinguished *prerational morality* as simply the "non-dialectical, casual, impulsive, polyglot" satisfaction of preferences as they occur.[21] But the preferences and needs of an individual may obviously conflict with one another and with those of other men. Consequently the impulse to rationality is not only one need among many to be satisfied on its own account but also a means to the fulfillment of other needs and preferences and to a measure of harmony among them. "It is *prudent* to be rational up to a certain point, because if we neglect too many or too deeply rooted impulses in ourselves or in the world, our master-passion itself will come to grief."[22] The primary function of reason in morals then is not in the least to define the good or to deny that certain things are desirable or that certain desires are right. The moral function of reason is to satisfy the "demand that life be consistent, complete, and satisfactory when reflected upon and viewed as a whole."[23] Therefore the chief requirement of rational morality is, as Socrates insisted, self-knowledge; for "right conscience in a natural creature can be nothing but self-knowledge, by which the man discovers his own nature and the good on which it is set."[24] So the aim of reason in morals is also not primarily to alter desires or needs. "Morality becomes rational precisely by refusing either to accept human nature, as it sprouts, altogether without harmony, or to mutilate it in the haste to make it harmonious."[25] Happiness, as the only justification of existence, must be the aim of rationality in morals. "Happiness is the only sanction of life; where happiness fails, existence remains a mad and lamentable experiment."[26] Happiness, however, is not easily achieved. "Happiness implies resource and security; it can be achieved only by discipline. . . . Discipline discredits the random pleasures of illusion, hope, and triumph, and substitutes those which are self-reproductive, perennial, and serene, because they express an equilibrium maintained with reality."[27] Self-knowledge and the pursuit of happiness become therefore the only basis in a rational life for accepting, rejecting, or modifying the impulses, preferences, tendencies, and needs that life may spontaneously generate. A life of reason is a life based on self-knowledge in the pursuit of happiness. And if the aims of rational morality could wholly succeed, nothing truly desired or needed for happiness, whether material or spiritual, would have to be renounced or sacrificed.

But neither man nor the world, Santayana was convinced, is wholly rational. Consequently the most careful and persistent attempts to live rationally may fail in one particular or another. When this happens men may forsake reason or the attempt to achieve harmony among various impulses and needs through rational discipline and seek happiness miraculously by appealing to some more or less dominant aspect of experience as the only genuine clue to goodness or salvation. This is *postrational morality*. The results of such postrational schemes—including Epicureanism, Stoicism, and Christianity—has, he thought, been chiefly "to console or deceive the soul with some substitute for happiness."[28] Yet such substitutes for reason and happiness, he admitted, are not wholly or simply willful and gratuitous. "These systems are a refuge from an intolerable situation: they are experiments in redemption."[29] The founders of such systems suppose, though without good reasons, "that by estranging oneself from the world, or resting in the moment's pleasure, or mortifying the passions, or enduring all sufferings in patience, or studying a perfect conformity with the course of affairs, one may gain admission to some sort of residual mystical paradise; and this thought, once conceived, is published as a revelation and accepted as a panacea."[30] Although postrational moralities are self-contradictory, in that they must inevitably call reason to the defense of systems that also deny the worth of reason, they are not altogether without positive value. For "certain rare and precious virtues can be thus inaugurated,"[31] and although they constitute no genuine advance in either self-knowledge or self-discipline and offer no sound solutions to moral and spiritual problems, such systems may nonetheless both preserve some normal impulses from natural and rational systems of thought and so provide "the starting-point for a restored natural morality."[32]

There are apparently two crucial (and closely related) difficulties in Santayana's account and analysis of moral experience and judgment. The first is the denial that moral judgments can be true or false except in a very weak and conventional sense dictated by usage.[33] Although this view has become quite common among the positivists and linguistic analysts, the difficulties have not been significantly mitigated by greater popularity. There is indeed a striking similarity between the positivists' claim that all value judgments are emotive and cognitively meaningless because they cannot be empirically verified and Santayana's argument. "The cry, *How beautiful!* or *How good!* may be sincere, and it may be applauded," he wrote, "but it is never true." At least, he insisted, it can never be true except *morally*. And being *morally true,* he thought, is significantly different from being *really* or *actually* true. For if everyone agrees, he argued, "the judgment will then be true morally: that is, it will express the bias of human nature."[34] Therefore when he claimed that "To reach moral truth, which like all truth is eternal, we should have to remember or foresee with absolute clearness the aspirations of all souls at all moments; and confronting these aspirations with their occasions, we should have to measure their relative vanity and physical compatibility," he must have meant only an ideal that is impossible to achieve—a harmony or "truth" that is eternal only because it is ideal or nonexistent. A moral judgment is not true in any radical sense, he clearly believed, because "there seems to be no conceivable object or reality in reference to which any type of morality could be called true." Consequently he concluded that "Such moral rightness [as is usually claimed] in moral sentiment is either a tautology, meaning that you prize what you prize, or want what you want, or it is a tangle of confusion."[35]

But surely the "tangle of confusion" is not at all avoided by the denial of truth in a radical sense to moral judgments. Indeed to suppose that truth is possible only in reference to some independent object or reality is already to introduce strains and stringencies that no serious theory of truth can tolerate. For such a view makes it impossible to say, for example, either that arithmetic is true or that it is true that a child is potentially a man. For arithmetic and statements about potentiality do not indicate independent objects or realities (at least in Santayana's sense) against which truth claims can be tested. But surely *truth* need imply only, as Santayana himself often recognized, that claims are trustworthy; furthermore, judgments may take the form of actions and products as well as verbal claims. Thus truth may be said to sustain and guide as well as point. And there can be little doubt that moral judgments—though often a great deal of variability is possible and permissible in them—are among the most necessary, dependable, and precious elements of man's heritage. Also to deny moral truth or the truth of value judgments and yet insist that "value is the principle of perspective in science" as well as morals is in effect to dismiss the pursuit of truth as totally futile.

But the more basic difficulty, and incidentally one that Santayana shared with many other moral philosophers, lies in the assumption that all truth about preference, and consequently about all goodness and moral judgment, is completely relative to *a nature* that can presumably be discovered in mankind and in each individual. In terms of this supposed nature both *what is* and *what ought to be* can presumably be found out or discovered. But to be consistent this theory must also claim that a man's understanding and evaluation of the demands of his own nature and knowledge are inescapably conditioned by his own nature, and so on *ad infinitum.* So if man is never essentially an *openness to the world,* aware not only of quantitative facts and relations but also of his own powers, virtues, faults, and failures as they really are, then surely all forms of judgment are perhaps equally dubious and presumptuous. But if the mind is, as Aristotle said, pure potentiality in the sense that it may become whatever it knows, then there is no insurmountable difficulty in the pursuit of knowledge, whether scientific or moral. In other words, either knowledge that is radically unconditioned is possible, in which case moral as well as scientific standards may be wisely and truly chosen, or there is no point at all in attempting to determine what man's nature is and requires.

And on this analysis one can suggest that Bertrand Russell was evidently closest to the truth about the foundation of morals when he held with G. E. Moore that the good is no more dependent on man's nature or knowledge than round or square is. Or as Moore himself suggested, it seems quite plausible that a beautiful world—orderly, harmonious, symmetrical, colorful—is indeed better than an ugly one—messy, in conflict with itself, chaotic, gray—even though there be no one to observe either. And if, as Santayana claimed, such a view has "the twang of intolerance and self-mutilation," while relativity "would tend to render people more truly social than would a belief that things have intrinsic and unchangeable values,"[36] this may be at least partly because the good, clearly seen, demands enormous efforts and sacrifices that only a few are willing and able to make. But surely there is no necessary relation between seeing that the good is objective and the attempt to force others to agree. And even if Santayana was right, as he apparently was, in claiming that "No form of life can be inherently wrong," the reason he gave—that "there is no criterion by which to judge except the inherent direction of life"[37]—is nonetheless superficial and irrelevant to moral judgment and behavior and certainly does not imply that a genuinely rational creature is equally justified in choosing simply any harmonious or satisfying course of action. For the fact that a form of life cannot be "inherently wrong" does not necessarily mean that no form or instance of thought and action can be wrong. Furthermore, there is apparently no "inherent direction" in man's life. Instead, he is radically free. Each action is apparently a selection from a field of preferences, all certainly if not equally eligible until eliminated by choice or time. Moral judgment or decision seems at least to discriminate between the features of an objective situation rather than merely to actualize the inevitable attitude and direction of organic potentiality and process.

There seems in any case to be more hope as well as more consistency, internally and with the facts of experience, in the claim that truth about the good as well as truth about quantitative facts and relations is possible. For any approach that begins by declaring that preference is the ultimate basis of all good and that preference is itself produced finally by the blind nature or machinery of the body is completely frustrated by its own logic even before it begins. This was recognized at least implicitly by William James when he insisted, in "The Moral Philosopher and the Moral Life," that "Whether a God exist, or no God exist . . . we form at any rate an ethical republic here below" and went on to suggest that God is morally significant as "a pretext for living hard, and getting out of the game of existence its keenest possibilities of dezest." So to conceive the demands of morality as the demands of God, James thought, is to claim that reality as such demands a strenuous ethic of "infinite and mysterious obligation" or that nature is not indifferent and that a genial morality of "prudence and the satisfaction of merely finite need" is not enough. Theism, according to James, is thus a form of the necessary recognition that moral values and action are significant not only in the life of individuals and groups but also in the universe as a whole or without strict temporal and spatial limits.[38] And although John Dewey's theory of the good, and of moral action, suffers in some respects from a naturalistic relativity not so very different from that of Santayana, he also was sounder and more consistent in that he claimed that *if* qualities, such as goods and bads, as reflected in acceptances and rejections, means and ends, "characterize nature, then they manifest themselves in the uses, enjoyments and sufferings, the searchings and strivings which form conscious experience. These are as realistic, as 'objectively' natural, as are the constituents of the object of cognitional experience."[39] He thus admits no radical distinction between the experiential and existential status of "goods" and "facts," of "value" and "existence." In both James and Dewey existence is itself clearly and radically *moral* in a sense that Santayana most emphatically denied.

Santayana's *individualism*—a theory of the nature rather than the *worth* of individuals—was perhaps expressed most forcefully and unambiguously in his social and political philosophy. He frankly admitted that he thoroughly disliked modern trends in social theory and practice. Accordingly, in the "Preface" to *Dominations and Powers,* he remarked, "if one political tendency kindled my wrath, it was precisely the tendency of industrial liberalism to level down all civilisation to a single cheap and dreary pattern."[40] He had written similarly almost half a century earlier that "The ideal state and the ideal universe should be a family where all are not equal but where all are happy."[41] And this ideal is such, he thought, not only in the sense that it does not actually exist but also in the sense that it is presumably implicit in the actual character and relations of men. Each individual has his own powers and potentialities, and his happiness as well as his health and character lie in the appropriate use and development of these. Consequently not every individual can be expected to perform the same tasks or to be satisfied with the same kinds and degrees of privilege. The ideal state is then a monarchy and "an ideal monarchy is a many-coloured society. There is vital freedom for the individual, since a wise monarch recognises the inwardness, originality, and secrecy of each actual life." Therefore the wise monarch would also "maintain a hierarchy of offices and emoluments, as the Catholic Church does. . . . These would be given with an eye to the good of the whole people, and of the special service concerned."[42]

Yet Santayana recognized with Aristotle that the appearance of a monarch wise and good enough to govern beneficently is an altogether too rare and improbable event to make monarchy a truly dependable form of government. He did not, however, follow Aristotle to the conclusion that democracy is the best of the various forms of government that are actually possible. He had in fact little but scorn for the modern forms and aims of democracy. "If we bend the original meaning of the word to its present use," he wrote, "we may say that democracy is power exercised by the proletariat for its own benefit." And "proletariat," he added, "is an ugly word for an ugly thing. . . . The proletariat is the vast crowd of exiles in their own country whom the lure of industrial wages and town amusements has uprooted from their villages."[43] Modern democracy, in the pursuit of equality and freedom, he claimed, demands and produces unanimity—even though there can be genuine unanimity only in misery. The basic fault of democracy, he was convinced, is due finally to two false assumptions that rest in turn on a mistake in biology. The assumptions are "that human nature in all men is essentially similar, and that consequently mankind could not fully develop its vital liberty without coming to a unanimous vision of the world and a cooperative exercise of the same virtues."[44] Democracy attempts, in other words, to turn the wolf or the lion into a sheep; and this, he thought, is biologically impossible.

Therefore the way to moral progress, he suggested, is not democracy—indeed not anything social or moral at all—but rather "inbreeding, which allows the special potentialities in one incipient variety of human beings to develop."[45] Such a view of the ground and method of moral progress is of course consistent with thoroughgoing materialism and with the notion that "freedom of mind depends on freedom to rearrange material conditions so that, living under them, the mind may flourish effectually."[46] Although there is a paradox in supposing that mind can manipulate at all the material elements on which it is completely dependent, there would be freedom in this arrangement for those—if any—who had the power to order things to their own advantage. The view is also consistent with the claim that the only possible wisdom in the idea that one knows what is good for others must be based on acquaintance with "the difficulties and the failures that external and persistent circumstances prepare for the unwary."[47] No one, he thought, can know the desires and ideals or the spiritual values and needs of another person or choose the good life for him. For this reason the duties of government as he conceived it are severely limited. A good government will "see that the people have enough to eat," "regulate population," provide defense, and "facilitate prosperity" by providing such things as roads and bridges.[48] In other words, "Government is an art, serving economic and moral interests. . . . Mankind walks on one material planet under one material firmament; these conditions it is to their common advantage to respect. But, that toll once paid to necessity, why should not vital liberty in each heart devise the private or social or ideal order by which it would live."[49]

Recognizing the improbability of beneficent monarchy and despising both the form and the fruit of radical democracy, Santayana suggested in *Reason in Society* that the best of the possible forms of government would be *timocracy*. He described timocracy as "a government by men of merit."[50] A timocracy would combine the advantages and avoid the faults of various other forms of government:

> People would be born equal, but they would grow unequal, and the only equality subsisting would be equality of opportunity. . . . It would promote freedom scientifically. . . . Like aristocracy, it would display a great diversity of institutions and superposed classes, a stimulating variety in ways of living. . . . Like social democracy, finally, it would be just and open to every man, but it would not depress hu-

manity nor wish to cast everybody in a common mould.[51]

Timocracy, he claimed, would represent the ideal of reason, a perfect combination of order and liberty. It would provide not only the necessary skill and intelligence but also eminence in government. And eminence, whether the government is composed of one or several men, is desirable, he claimed, because it is synthetic and therefore representative of the hopes and aspirations of the people. "Excellence in anything," he argued, "whether thought, action, or feeling, consists of nothing but representation, in standing for many different constituents reduced to harmony, so that the wise moment is filled with an activity just to all extant interests and speaking in their total behalf."[52] Eminent men in government would thus *represent* the true and inward hopes of mankind. And democratic government as now constituted, he suggested, is made possible only by the fact that truly eminent men are no longer trusted. Yet only the influence of eminent men—traditionally the influence of an aristocracy—he claimed, has lifted mankind "above a dead level of infinite dullness and vulgarity." Without this influence, he asked rhetorically, "Would mankind be anything but a trivial, sensuous, superstitious, custom-ridden herd?"[53]

Although there is no mention of timocracy in *Dominations and Powers,* clearly Santayana's ideal of individual liberty and the social order did not change greatly. A government that aspires to be rational, he wrote in the later book, must "imitate the modesty of the physician that recommends only what can enable us to escape or to overcome the assaults that natural accidents may make upon us. . . . All else a rational government would leave to the special genius of each free society and each free individual."[54] He admitted that perhaps only a "thorough levelling and kneading" could eliminate the "gratuitous violence and madness that now infect mankind. "But then," he added, "from that blameless and level lawn that would cover the planet, somewhere one blade of grass would have to grow into a fern and another into a tree, if that varied and tragic flora that we call civilisation were ever to arise again."[55]

Timocracy as Santayana conceived it, although he himself no doubt thought otherwise, is obviously identical in certain respects with the social and political ideals often cherished, particularly by Americans, in the name of democracy. Yet even as neither common sense nor philosophic thought in America has assumed that moral ideals are primarily physical or biological in origin, so neither has seen any genuine threat to civilization or to genuine moral and spiritual excellence in democratic institutions and social equality. For a man is apparently not simply enclosed in and propelled by the elaborate machinery of the body but is rather sensitive or open to the detailed vastness of the world around him. And if this is the case, there cannot be the sharp distinction between the individual and society or between personal liberty and public policy that Santayana evidently assumed. The social environment is apparently no less important than biological structure and potentiality to personal excellence. And surely social and moral democracy need not imply in the least either the mediocrity of the individual or an identity of needs and achievements; its main points are the intrinsic worth of each person and the equality or dignity implied thereby. In the last analysis Santayana's ideals and fears seem more properly relevant to a program of animal breeding, designed to produce superiority in mere size or brute strength, than to the achievement of a political order favorable to excellence in the genuinely moral and intellectual dimensions of man.

Chapter 9

ART, BEAUTY, MEANING, AND VALUE

". . . the effort of art is to keep what is interesting in existence, to recreate it in the eternal."

Reason in Art

No doubt one of the most distinctive features of George Santayana's philosophy, particularly in comparison with that of his contemporaries, was the great and central importance he attached to the arts and the experience of beauty. Certainly no other contemporary American philosopher, and probably none in another time and place, has made art so indicative of the nature and status of all knowledge and understanding or beauty so central among the values of existence. His first important philosophical work was *The Sense of Beauty,* a study, as he described it, of "those fundamental aesthetic feelings the orderly extension of which yields sanity of judgment and distinction of taste."[1] And among the five volumes of *The Life of Reason* no other volume, with the possible exception of *Reason in Religion,* was as clearly conceived and as sharply focused as was *Reason in Art.* And in later life his estimate of the character and importance of art and beauty did not change greatly, although after he became preoccupied with the more speculative themes of *Realms of Being* and with social and political theory, he wrote about them only incidentally. "In order to obtain anything lovely," he said in *Dominations and Powers,* "I would gladly extirpate all the crawling ugliness in the world," and went on in the same paragraph to suggest that "concern about the causes and the enemies of the beautiful" was one of the chief motivations in his study of social orders and political powers.[2]

The traditional and notorious neglect of artistic principles and aesthetic values by philosophers has been due in part clearly to the conviction that the cultivation of art is not only the cultivation of illusion but also inevitably involves the neglect of more urgent, serious, and intellectually rewarding matters. Ever since Plato suggested in *The Republic* that the artist, because he copies material objects that are themselves only poor imitations of the eternal idea, is thrice removed from reality and therefore engrossed in an activity that corrupts the soul with illusions, philosophers have often found the arts suspect or at least less than the most serious and successful way of coping with the actual problems of existence. And it is surely significant that Santayana in some measure found the arts so important and congenial for the very same reasons that many others ignored them or found them misleading and demoralizing. He agreed that the arts are concerned with illusions, but thought that Plato had grossly "overestimated the influence which art can have on character and affairs."[3] Therefore, unlike the existentialist philosophers, who in recent years have seriously turned to the arts—particularly to the novel and drama—in order to articulate better certain supposedly crucial aspects or qualities of existence, Santayana valued the arts partly, or perhaps even mainly, because artistic forms and perspectives are essentially illusory. "Facts for a living creature," he said, "are only instruments; his play-life is his true life."[4] The fine arts especially belong significantly to the play-life of man. And in a world and among creatures where, as he thought, the illusions of play-life so often parade (particularly in the name of religion) as the most important realities, there is a special value in the illusions that encourage and sustain play and yet profess to be nothing but illusions.

Of course Santayana never suggested that illusions constitute the whole of artistic or aesthetic value. Art, like religion and science, is also a form of reason—even the fundamental form of reason insofar as all judgment involves techniques and interpretation or a disciplined method and imagination. The values of art and beauty are in themselves extraordinary but they also signify, even if they do not seriously alter, other important features of man's existence. "Art springs so completely from the heart of man that it makes everything speak to him in his own language; it reaches, nevertheless, so truly to the heart of nature that it cooperates with her, becomes a parcel of her creative material energy, and builds by her instinctive hand."[5] Furthermore, "Beauty is a pledge of the possible conformity between the soul and nature, and consequently a ground of faith in the supremacy of the good."[6] There was then no deliberate exaggeration when he claimed, "Of all reason's embodiments art is therefore the most splendid and complete."[7] But presumably this account of art as an extraordinary form of reason does not contradict the claim that art is essentially illusory or in Santayana's own words that there exists "nothing in nature *like* these moral or sensuous fictions" of the poet or the prophet. There is no contradiction because "there is necessarily in nature some contact or nexus which those fictions express and report."[8]

Yet Santayana has sometimes been called an "aesthete" and his philosophy "aesthetic," suggesting generally, and with disapproval, that he was interested primarily if not exclusively in the illusion itself, in beauty or form alone, and not at all seriously in the intelligibility and uses of things. Much as he valued formal and sensuous qualities for their beauty and despaired of knowing what so many men have claimed to know about the causal order, this view is nonetheless profoundly erroneous and quite unfair to his conception of philosophy as well as to his total approach to artistic and aesthetic values. This is made clearest perhaps in *Reason in Art.* "To separate the aesthetic element, abstract and dependent as it often is," he said, "is an artifice which is more misleading than helpful; for neither in the history of art nor in a rational estimate of its value can the aesthetic function of things be divorced from the practical and moral." Or in metaphorical and perhaps more emphatic terms, "The rose's grace," he added, "could more easily be plucked from its petals than the beauty of art from its subject, occasion, and use." And in a different metaphor, "The aesthetic good will be . . . hatched in the same nest with the others, and incapable of flying far in a different air."[9] Indeed in his most fundamental and broadest use of the term, he meant by "art," as the Greeks did by *"technē,"* only a deliberate and successful method, a technique, a form of discipline, or reason itself. In this sense, "The arts are evidences of wisdom, and sources of it; they include science"[10] and "progress is art bettering the conditions of existence."[11] But of course he also meant by "art" the "fine" or "liberal" arts and concentrated on these in certain volumes and extensive parts of his various works. And the concern of this chapter is mainly the fine or liberal rather than the industrial arts. The distinction between these two forms, directions, or aspects of art, though not absolute, is explicit and is best expressed in his own terms:

> There are two directions in which it seems fitting that rational art should proceed. . . . Art may come to buttress a particular form of life, or it may come to express it. All that we call industry, science, business, morality buttresses our life; it informs us about our conditions and adjusts us to them; it equips us for life; it lays out the ground for the game we are to play. This preliminary labour, however, need not be servile. To do it is also to exercise our faculties; and in that exercise our faculties may grow free,—as the imagination of Lucretius, in tracing the course of the atoms, dances and soars most congenially. One extension of art then would be in the direction of doing artistically, joyfully, sympathetically, whatever we have to do. . . .
>
> There remains a second form of rational art, that of expressing the ideal towards which we would move under these improved conditions. . . . The outer life is for the sake of the inner; discipline is for the sake of freedom, and conquest for the sake of self-possession. This inner life is wonderfully redundant; there is, namely, very much more in it than a consciousness of those acts by which the body

> adjusts itself to its surroundings . . . each sense has its arbitrary quality, each language its arbitrary euphony and prosody; each game has its creative laws, every soul its own tender reverberations and secret dreams. Life has a margin of play which might grow broader, if the sustaining nucleus were more firmly established in the world. To the art of working well a civilised race would add the art of playing well. To play with nature and make it decorative, to play with the overtones of life and make them delightful, is a sort of art. It is the ultimate, the most artistic sort of art, but it will never be practiced successfully as long as the other sort of art is in a backward state; for if we do not know our environment, we shall mistake our dreams for a part of it, and so spoil our science by making it fantastic, and our dreams by making them obligatory.[12]

Of course one of the fundamental *values* of art is beauty; beauty is, however, nonetheless only an incidental *aim* of art. So although he said that "Maxims in art are pernicious; beauty is here the only commandment," he also added almost immediately that "Beauty is adventitious, occasional, incidental in human products no less than in nature."[13]

Santayana's conviction that beauty is neither the basic aim nor the most important value in art was no doubt closely related to his criticism of "art for art's sake" and "museum art." He claimed that "nothing is really so poor as art that is interested in itself and not in its subject"[14] and more specifically "that there is nothing which so quickly discredits itself as empty rhetoric and dialectic, or poetry that wanders in dim and private worlds."[15] For genuine art, he thought, must grow out of and express ideals that are directly relevant to human conditions, to man's needs and potentialities. "Artificial art, made to be exhibited, is something gratuitous and sophisticated, and the greatest part of men's concern about it is affectation."[16] He called this approach to art "aestheticism" and indicated that he regarded it, not at all as a rational form of art, but as a serious deviation from the concern and practice of serious artists, who work "under the patronage of industry, religion, custom, sentiment or pride" and who "are not aesthetes" but craftsmen.[17] "Aestheticism," he said in obvious disapproval, "is a refined sensuality, the gift of finding an immediate joy in the obvious,"[18] and "the aesthete is essentially an amateur, a poetic spirit listening rather than composing. But in the modern world, where nobody knows where he belongs, it has occurred to him to pose as an artist." However, the fact that the aesthete poses as an artist also has social causes and an ulterior purpose. "He would blush to confess himself a mere aesthete coming to be ministered to and not to minister; he wishes to prove that he has a public function, and to justify his existence by doing some work, no matter how bad or unnecessary." Such merely aesthetic interest, Santayana claimed, whether formal or sensuous, is an unstable perversion of the integral role that art and beauty should normally assume in the rational life. "A workman can hardly be true to a merely aesthetic fancy; it melts into something different; often it has sickened him before his apprentices have had time to adopt it." As full of contempt as these words obviously are, his harshest judgments of the aesthete and aestheticism came later in *Dominations and Powers* as part of a section on the "Dissolution of the Arts":

> The aesthete armed with his supercilious sensibility and transcendental freedom, intrudes into the workshop of the arts with his nose in the air; but he remains an amateur in his craft, plays a game of bluff with the public (a game which for a time is often successful), but dwindles and soon vanishes from the scene in consequence of his inherent vacuity. For the arts, after all, draw their life-blood from a well-digested craftsman's tradition. But the aesthete, posing in his studio, despises his masters, if he ever had them, and flits from one experiment to another until

perhaps his extravagances bring him round full circle to the most primitive conventions.[19]

The public, he continued, must of course share the blame for this "dissolution of the arts" into a superficial aestheticism. For the evidence of aestheticism among the public and the causes of it in the aesthete include the practice of collecting and exhibiting art in museums. Museums are truly valuable, he suggested, only for the historian. "A genuine lover of the beautiful would never enter a museum."[20] He had been only a bit more generous earlier. "An artist may visit a museum," he wrote in *Reason in Art,* "but only a pedant can live there."[21] The point of these intemperate words, if such they are, is that art, although basically and even inevitably illusory, has essential connections and relations among the vital and spiritual needs of life; the emphasis on aesthetic surface or formal values alone, he was convinced, must ignore and ultimately undermine and destroy the very conditions that make art possible.

Yet Santayana was by no means as unsympathetic to beauty or the aesthetic experience as the quotations above, separated from the context of his work, might suggest. In *Interpretations of Poetry and Religion* he wrote, "The aesthetic attitude is not the moral, but it is not for that reason illegitimate. It gives us refreshment and a foretaste of that perfect adaptation of things to our faculties and of our faculties to things which, could it extend to every part of experience, would constitute the ideal life."[22] He had already written in *The Sense of Beauty* (in addition to the quote above about beauty being the basis of faith in the good) that the imaginative attempt to remove all evil from life leaves "little but aesthetic pleasure remaining to constitute unalloyed happiness. Even the knowledge of truth, which the most sober theologians made the essence of the beatific vision, is an aesthetic delight: for when the truth has no further practical utility, it becomes a landscape. The delight of it is imaginative and the value of it aesthetic."[23] He also suggested in the same work that no element or aspect of existence demands a higher estimate of worth than the experience of beauty. "To feel beauty," he wrote, "is a better thing than to understand how we come to feel it, to have imagination and taste, to love the best, to be carried by the contemplation of nature to a vivid faith in the ideal, all this is more, a great deal more, than any science can hope to be."[24] And many years later he indicated that whereas he had formerly, particularly in *Reason in Art,* regarded the moral burden of poetry as indispensable, he had finally concluded that there is indeed sufficient value in "mere grace and feeling and music and cloud-castles and frolic."[25] There can then be no doubt that he always placed beauty among the highest and most significant values. Yet beauty itself, he thought, must signify vital harmonies and ideals appropriate to a particular form of life. Otherwise it may distort and confuse man's spirit at its source and so become a great deal less than the unmitigated good it is capable of being. This was emphasized finally in *Dominations and Powers* where he said that even "as the beautiful is a mark of vital perfection, and life everywhere, if it can, perfects its movements, there is potential beauty of all sorts in the world."[26] But the potential beauties can be actualized, he was convinced, not by seeking for beauty as such, but only by perfecting the complex conditions on which the experience of it depends.

Beauty cannot, Santayana thought, be regarded as the fundamental value or the basic aim of even the fine arts. "The fine arts are butter to man's daily bread; there is no conceiving or creating them except as they spring out of social exigencies."[27] Yet certainly the fine arts are not to be regarded as practical, at least not in the common and narrow connotations of the term. Practical needs are satisfied by the industrial forms of art. The fine arts, he obviously believed, are primarily ways of expressing and realizing the *meaning* of experience—when *meaning* refers primarily to the recognition of certain momentous qualities, values, or relations that add great importance and depth to the presence of what is otherwise unimportant and thin. Thus painting, for example, is not primarily the production of an aesthetic object. "To paint," he said, "is a way of letting vision work."[28] The emphasis here is apparently on *work*. Painting is then a way of apprehending and communicating the significant features of things that only painting can reveal and that are humanly important; for "art, after all, exists for the mind and must speak humanly."[29] Similarly, if literature is to speak humanly, "it cannot long forget . . . that it serves a burdened and perplexed creature, a human animal struggling to persuade the universal Sphinx to propose a more intelligible riddle."[30]

Consequently grimace and gesture, he suggested, may be regarded as the primitive paradigms of the nature and functions of the arts; they have their origin in the automatic behavior of the organism and their justification in their function. They are also modified by their own effects and so "become artful and . . . transform their automatic expressiveness into ideal expression."[31] Thus grimace and gesture become forms of rational expression or signs of intent and importance. For by revealing intentions and states of mind they acquire meanings and functions which action alone could rarely or never have or fulfill. Music, Santayana suggested, originates and develops in much the same way; it begins in a "need of exercise and self-expression" and becomes the purest of the arts in which nonetheless "a thousand shades of what, in our blundering words, we call sadness or mirth, find . . . their distinct expression." It is therefore the "singular privilege" of music "to give form to what is naturally inarticulate, and express those depths of human nature which can speak no language current in the world." For this reason presumably "we dance, pray, and mourn to music, and the more inadequate words or external acts are to the situation, the more grateful music is."[32] The value of music is then not merely aesthetic or sensuous and formal but rational; for it expresses the strains and predicaments of human existence.

Similarly the poet, by "prompting mankind to imagine," helps men to live; he presents "in graphic images the total efficacy of things" and so represents "more thoroughly than any formula the concrete burden of experience."[33] The rational poet is one who perceives the "wonder, pathos, and beauty" of the things around him and "presents his subject loaded with its whole fate, missing no source of worth which is in it, no ideal influence which it may have." Through poetry man's "ultimate interests" may "speak eloquently to the soul."[34] Likewise painting and sculpture, although valuable simply because they provide the "sense of victory and dominion" which may come from leaving "at least the temporary stamp of one's special will on the world,"[35] may also please both aesthetically and intellectually. Through form and color and their powers of suggestion painting and sculpture become modes of expressing satirical intentions and philosophical ideas as well as certain moods and the love of sensuous qualities. The greatest achievements of such arts are then by no means immediately available to the eye. "The Venus of Milo will not seem beautiful, in any deep sense, to anyone incapable of feeling the luminous scorn, the victorious perfection of the Greek immortals."[36] In summary, according to Santayana, art speaks primarily to and for the intellect or spirit rather than to and for the senses, or is a spiritual rather than an aesthetic or practical good. "The noblest art will be the one, whether plastic or literary or dialectical, which creates figments most truly representative of what is momentous in human life."[37]

Precisely because art is presumably an expression of the conditions and ideals of life, and thus a possible embodiment of reason, Santayana thought it must and can be justified philosophically. Only on a prerational level, he said, can art be "prized as something supreme and irresponsible"[38] or for its own sake alone. Yet it would be utterly inaccurate to suggest that he thought the arts should be subordinate to, or subject to summary judgments in terms of, moral, economic, or religious interests and convictions. None of these can speak with authority about the nature and place of the arts in man's life. Art is nonetheless only one part of life and must exist in harmony with other important interests and activities. Happiness and civilization, indeed, are attained and measured, he suggested, only "by the proportion of its energy which is devoted to free and generous pursuits, to the adornment of life and the culture of the imagination. For it is in the spontaneous play of his faculties that man finds himself and his happiness."[39] Therefore, far from suggesting that art is intrinsically subject to judgment by moral criteria, he claimed that when the state is at last reasonably ordered "questions of art will be the most urgent questions of morals, . . . genius at last will feel responsible, and the twist given to imagination will seem the most crucial thing in life."[40]

The justification of life, Santayana of course believed, must be intrinsic, a pervasive quality that makes living a good in itself. Art must then also be justified by contributing to the total quality that makes life intrinsically worth having. It may do this in several ways. One is by recasting "in idea a world which we have no present means of recasting in reality." Another way is by renewing vision and creating a fresh world in fancy "where all form has the same inner justification that all life has in the real world. . . . Art supplies constantly to contemplation what nature seldom affords in concrete experience—the union of life and peace."[41] More specifically, "Forms of poetry are forms of human life. Languages express national character and enshrine particular ways of seeing and valuing events."[42] Also the arts may turn moral and aesthetic evils into "pathetic and magnificent harmonies" and so help to achieve that "aesthetic sanction" that "sweetens all successful living."[43]

Artistic and aesthetic values, though clearly not intrinsically moral or subject to moral judgment, are nonetheless clearly related to moral values in two important respects. First, the fine arts, as the freest and highest expressions of the human spirit, are among the most necessary and precious fulfillments of man's potential. As such the arts are of course goods and it is immoral to forbid their development and distribution. But the arts also have moral implications, as already suggested, as parts of a total life; as such they must be consistent with the complex conditions that make life possible and harmonious. Therefore, "We often come upon beauties that need to be sacrificed, as we come upon events and practical necessities without number that are truly regrettable."[44] There is then no fundamental difference between the moral status of artistic or aesthetic impulses and other basic propensities and goods. "Every impulse, not the aesthetic mood alone, is innocent and irresponsible in its origin and precious in its own eyes; but every impulse or indulgence, including the aesthetic, is evil in effect when it renders harmony impossible in the general tenor of life, or produces in the soul division and ruin."[45] If man's life were not subject to enormous dangers—to distraction, hunger, exposure, and innumerable conflicts of interest that confuse and hinder the spirit—or if the spirit were radically free rather than so completely dependent on complex material harmonies, no moral necessities or negative injunctions would need be imposed and the arts could be thoroughly fanciful and irresponsible. But in the actual conditions of existence, more fundamental and necessary—though not more important—matters may demand first and most careful attention.

So although the artistic spirit may aspire to be completely free of moral commitments and the impediments of practical affairs, or to enjoy the pure immediacy of image and sound and idea without alloy or interruption, life is in fact such that this ideal—if seriously pursued as an actual possibility—is illusory and therefore dangerous; for such attempts must ignore the infinite complexity of life and confuse a single good with the total harmony that life must have in order to be intrinsically valuable. So finally, "To criticise art on moral grounds is to pay it a high compliment by assuming that it aims to be adequate, and is addressed to a comprehensive mind. The only way art could disallow such criticism would be to protest its irresponsible infancy, and admit that it was a more or less amiable blatancy in individuals, and not art at all."[46]

The arts may also of course be judged aesthetically or artistically or in terms of certain standards and criteria of taste. But standards in art and taste, Santayana claimed, like standards in morals, are relative to historical ages and cultures and to individuals. Yet he noted certain factors that taste in any "deliberate and circumspect form" would presumably admit as relevant. These include the recognition of authorities such as the ancient Greeks who must be regarded as experts because of their great and obvious love of beauty. Also the specific technical values of any specific art are important, he thought, because they are "more permanent and definite than the adventitious analogies on which a stray observer usually bases his views." Therefore, "What painters say about painting and poets about poetry is better than lay opinion."[47] There are also, he suggested, certain representative and universal values that "have a normal aesthetic value"; these include "the human figure, elementary passions, common types and crises of fate" as well as "ultimate truths, cosmic laws, great human ideals."[48] But the fundamental point in artistic judgment, whether the judgment is aesthetically or morally based, is that "Good taste is that taste which is a good possession, a friend to the whole man. It must not alienate him from anything except to ally him to something greater and more fertile in satisfactions."[49] For "the whole man" is the necessary condition for the existence of the various powers of sense, imagination, reason, and spirit; presumably the life in which all these function harmoniously will be not only more complex but also richer and more satisfying than the life in which some are cultivated at the expense of others; "and the richer and more complex the organism that attains perfection, the more glorious its perfection will be. . . ."[50] But except for accidental harmonies and the felicity of nature such perfection can be approached, if at all, only through reason. If the aims of art and reason are the same, both are essentially methods of making certain values as pervasive and secure as the flux of nature will allow. Consequently, "An intelligent critic must look impartially to beauty, propriety, difficulty, originality, truth, and moral significance in the work he judges"[51] and "rational severity in respect to art simply weeds the garden; it expresses a mature aesthetic choice and opens the way to supreme artistic achievements. To keep beauty in its place is to make all things beautiful."[52] And if life were truly rational, the arts would express reality—or at least its significance for man—and the distinction between the fine and industrial arts would completely disappear. "All arts would be practiced together and merged in the art of life, the only one wholly useful or fine among them."[53]

The limits that Santayana would impose on the arts in order to make them rational no doubt appear stringent and unnecessary to many contemporary artists and critics. Why indeed, they may very reasonably ask, should the activities and products of the creative imagination be censured because they do not express the conditions and ideals of men at a particular time and place? Why deny the artist complete freedom to explore sensuous and formal as well as ideational possibilities in any direction in which his talents, energies, and materials allow? Why demand that artistic methods or products be harmonious with other, perhaps equally arbitrary and less valuable, practices or needs? For who can tell in what direction the great and significant artistic discoveries or creations and rewards lie?

And indeed it seems fairly clear that in the arts as in morals, perhaps partly because he was anxious to avoid the faults of both complete relativity and the imposition of preconceived or *a priori* standards, Santayana made essentially the same mistake as the pragmatists and other Darwinian naturalists who have tried to find reliable standards of conduct and judgment in natural processes and relations. This approach can hardly fail to ignore the most impressive, if perhaps also the strangest, aspect of human existence: that no matter how deeply and inextricably rooted in the soil and a particular time and place, man may nonetheless transcend his temporal and spatial conditions. For he is also open or sensitive to, and sometimes profoundly interested in, forms and possibilities, relations and qualities that are apparently related to his own welfare or destiny only by the fact that he may know or discover them. Santayana claimed that "the subject matter of art is life, life as it actually is" and that "the function of art is to make life better."[54] But neither of these claims is strictly or even significantly true unless they are simply conventional tautologies. In any case the subject matter of art is not life any more than the subject matter of mathematics or physics is life, except in the broad and quite trivial sense in which anything discovered or known in any way is related to life. Likewise, the function of art is to make life better only in the way that any discovery or adventure—as in nuclear physics, symbolic logic, or mountain climbing—may make it better; if man is what he seems to be, his life is apparently made better—intrinsically better—only by increased scope or the degree to which he does transcend his temporal and spatial environment and needs to apprehend in some measure both the remote and the eternal. Santayana's philosophy was sometimes an eloquent recognition of precisely this fact. Yet his treatment of the arts, of all things, seems in important respects a denial of it.

Consequently the similarities in Santayana's view to the account of the arts by John Dewey, the only pragmatist among his contemporaries who wrote extensively on the arts, are striking and surprising. There are of course important differences also; but these are not nearly as great and fundamental as Santayana's professed contempt for pragmatism would suggest. Dewey emphasized, as did Santayana, that the function of art is to make available meanings that, in his terms, are "capable of immediately enjoyed possession"; he also agreed that in an intelligently ordered life or society the distinction between "fine" or "liberal" and "industrial" or "useful" art would disappear. "The only basic distinction is between bad art and good art, and this . . . applies equally to things of use and of beauty."[55] He also said that science is most properly regarded as an art and described art as "a process of making the world a different place in which to live."[56]

And it is at least interesting that Santayana said that art provides in contemplation "the union of life and peace" and Dewey remarked that " 'Repose in stimulation' characterizes art."[57] Although Dewey did not protest "aestheticism" and "museum art" as emphatically as Santayana did, he referred with obvious disapproval to "fine art: the production of buildings in the name of the art of architecture; of pictures in the name of the art of painting; of novels, dramas, etc. in the name of literary art; a production which in reality is largely a form of commercialized industry in production of a class of commodities that find their sale among well-to-do persons desirous of maintaining a conventionally approved status."[58] "Generally speaking," he said in disapproval of both, "the typical collector is the typical capitalist. For evidence of good standing in the realm of higher culture, he amasses paintings, statuary, and artistic *bijoux,* as his stocks and bonds certify to his standing in the economic world."[59]

The most obvious difference between the two accounts is that Dewey declared frankly that the arts are instrumental, or efficacious modes of producing and controlling qualities of experience. But Santayana, in spite of his emphasis on the arts as techniques or disciplines and embodiments of reason or ways of improving the conditions of existence, emphatically disagreed with the claim that they are also instruments or means. Surely the chief characteristic of the arts, he thought, is that they are essentially ends, the fruits and in no sense the roots or instruments of production. Dewey suggested that the naturalist has only two alternatives in respect to the arts: he must regard art as either "a continuation, by means of intelligent selection and arrangement, of natural tendencies of natural events; or art is a peculiar addition to nature springing from something dwelling exclusively within the breast of man. . . ."[60] As a teleologist and nondeterminist Dewey was convinced that only the former alternative can provide an intelligible account of the arts. This view no doubt has its own serious difficulties but they are not as obvious as those in the second alternative. And Santayana in effect endorsed the second; for as a determinist who denied all teleology and regarded qualities as ultimately secondary and illusory or irrelevant to the causal order of events, he had finally to treat the arts as the gratuitous and incidental effects of physical and biological arrangements and events. Art finally becomes merely a symbol (or more properly a sign) of reason or order in nature, including harmonious relations between the individual and the conditions of his existence. The pragmatic and naturalistic tendencies in his thought finally give way, in spite of the resulting incongruity, to resignation and spiritual contemplation.

Chapter 10

SUMMARY AND EVALUATION

> "After life is over and the world has gone up in smoke, what realities might the spirit in us still call its own without illusion save the form of those very illusions which have made up our story?"
>
> *The Last Puritan*

The thought of George Santayana must, as suggested earlier, be characterized finally as *a philosophy of ultimate disillusion.* In the last analysis, he claimed, neither the senses, nor science, nor art, nor religion, nor philosophy can provide any genuine or trustworthy clues to the ultimate character of existence. Both *the way to* and *the substance of* the only truth possible to man is then disillusion. Apparently his most fundamental and enduring aim was therefore to indicate in philosophic terms the perennial perplexity and the appropriate values of a creature that can escape from credulity and radical error only by way of disillusion. Indeed he professed frankly that he did not know or care much about causes and existence as such; he was interested rather in appearances—the ideas, images, ideals, or beauties—that existence may arouse in the minds of men.

In *Scepticism and Animal Faith,* in a passage already quoted in part, he described the three ways by which an honest mind may presumably escape, not appearance or illusion itself—for that is inescapable—but the fear of illusion. The first way is death. But death, since it only destroys man and neither explains nor redeems his predicament, is no genuine escape. The second way is to correct the errors of judgment that constitute illusion, or to substitute reliable and satisfactory beliefs for the unreliable and unsatisfactory. This, he suggested, is the normal effort when judgment is obviously mistaken. But critically regarded, he continued, no belief is ultimately justified except by "custom, comfort, and the accidental absence of doubt." But such pragmatic assurances, when they are possible, are not revelations of truth but only temporary satisfactions of need. This method is then no genuine haven for the scrupulously honest mind seeking wholeheartedly not to be deceived. The third, and the only critically defensible position, is therefore to admit that the illusion—including all ideas and appearances—is only illusion; for in this way the illusion is forbidden "to claim any sort of being but that which it obviously has; and then, whether it profits me or not, it will not deceive me." The only certainty is thus the moral certainty that no idea or appearance *ought* to be called *true* or regarded as truly representative of the character of existence. Only by such disillusion, he was convinced, can one be reasonably sure that he is not profoundly mistaken in his claims about the nature of existence.[1]

This philosophy of ultimate disillusion was always implicit (and indeed often explicit) in Santayana's earlier writings, including *The Life of Reason;* the moral and intellectual necessity of disillusion was the central theme of *Scepticism and Animal Faith* and one of the main premises that unified the four major categories of *Realms of Being*. For essence, as conceived in that work, is only the formal condition of appearance and in no sense existential; matter or the matrix of all existence never appears at all; spirit is only a witness of (and can never explain or fully understand) power as exemplified in the passing parade of essence; and truth, except for conventional and homespun varieties by which men live and perform their various functions, is merely an ideal that no one approaches and only a few entertain. "The senses are poets" and art, science, or religion based on them can result only in "imaginary figments" that are "always inconclusive and unstable." There can then be no truth based on sense experience. And the perspective of the rationalist, who assumes that scientific and philosophical systems are true insofar as their claims are "all-comprehensive and coherent," although a "congenial prospect" for egotism, must define truth, he said, as "harmony in dreams" and so is finally only "a metaphysical echo of human craving for sympathy and democratic comfort in agreeing with the majority."[2] The final problem then is not whether Santayana was a philosopher. There can be no doubt that he seriously criticized the philosophic claims of others and *sought truth*—even though in a tragically emasculated form—in philosophic terms, which is all that any philosopher can reasonably claim to do. The important question is whether this philosophy, based on ultimate disillusion, articulated important—at least partially if not wholly *true*—claims about the nature of knowledge and existence. Did he identify and illuminate actual and significant aspects of the arts, the religions, the sciences, and the various forms of philosophy?

It would of course be pointless to suggest that Santayana was significantly disillusioned in respect to the arts. By and large he simply shared the general opinion that the fine arts are not seriously or directly involved in the pursuit of knowledge and therefore do not attempt to express the truth. Any approach to the arts as indicative of the actual character of existence he labeled romanticism or religion. Indeed, as already noted, the high value he placed on the arts was due at least in some part to the very fact that they appear content to remain illusions; thus they make no claims that must be discounted in order to avoid deception.

Santayana's disillusion was clearly most complete, notorious, and personally distressing in regard to religion. In spite of the fact that he described his view of religion as "native to me and congenital,"[3] there was apparently nonetheless a good deal of agony in the conclusion that religions are essentially poetic and imaginative. Unlike many of his contemporaries, he was obviously not pleased by the thought that he must regard religions as so many fictions tragically mistaken for accounts of actual existence. This was perhaps due partly to the fact that, unlike many whose spiritual sympathies and vision are less developed or developed in different directions, he was unable to share the conviction that progress in science has made life intrinsically better or mitigated the moral and existential perplexities of man. That religion "has absolutely no standing ground in fact" and twists "the natural course of things into a moral fable"[4] did not suggest to him (as obviously it did to many of his contemporaries) that the world is ultimately more intelligible or more amenable to the understanding and control of man than religious men have generally supposed. The conclusion that religions are products of fancy and desperate hope, or at best "sensuous or imaginative signs" of "the real presence of pressing dangers and favourable opportunities,"[5] meant to him only that "the best things" do not exist. The lovely perspectives and images of the religions are specious, derivative, and altogether irrelevant to the causal order of nature. Yet no less than William James, he was aware of the apparent urgency and the great appeal of religious ideas and ideals. But although he obviously trusted the "dark fertility" of matter even more implicitly and perhaps with less reason than James trusted "some power not ourselves that makes for righteousness," he could not believe that religious symbols in any way indicate the character of reality. The apparent basis of this difference was that James, though an agnostic in many respects, began with the assumption that *no* experience can be completely misleading in regard to the character of existence while Santayana assumed that no experience is ever really trustworthy. So James suggested that religious experience may signify the ultimate fulfillment of human need and aspiration while Santayana concluded that the elemental darkness of all origins is symbolic of man's ultimate condition and destiny.

However, the great difference between Santayana and most other philosophers who have reached similar conclusions about the status of religious claims is that the others have, at least very often, been able to retain or substitute faith in science or philosophy or social reform for their discarded religious faith. Many of course have never really been tempted by religious attitudes and doctrines, or have simply dismissed religions as illusory without struggle or regret—though this may indeed have been possible only because they failed to see as deeply and broadly as Santayana did into the human sources and functions of religious ideas and practices. For although he professed to believe that the collocations and processes of matter are the ultimate condition and cause of all phenomena, including religious experience and ideas, his account of the nature and functions of religion is nonetheless an illuminating and suggestive inquiry into the actual conditions and needs of the human spirit. Disillusioned as he was, he was never tempted to dismiss religious claims and images as altogether *meaningless* or to suppose that in calling them *symbolic* he was distinguishing radically between the cognitive import of religion and science. But conversely, he clearly regarded as simply futile romanticism the effort, such as that of the existential phenomenologists, to discover ontological significance or truth in religious and poetic claims and experiences. The primacy of matter and the imaginative character of the arts and religions implied precisely that nothing existential—nothing with executive power or influence—can be discovered in or through the religious and artistic enterprises. But since life is not possible without illusion or a judicious life without disillusion, the intrinsic value of life must be measured in terms of the ideals of perfection that may occur in the imagination, and not in terms of the material powers and relations that make life possible and secure. Religions and the arts are meaningful, perhaps even the most meaningful of all man's activities and achievements, since without them all else would be means without ends—means that apparently would soon turn to ashes in the mouth. Those who dismiss religion as irrelevant to the meaning of existence are apt to think that through science or philosophy life can be lived and understood without illusion. Santayana regarded those who hold this belief as profoundly mistaken. For although they are right, he suggested, in supposing that religious visions and claims cannot be trusted in the pursuit of truth, they are wrong both in thinking that this is a serious impediment to their genuine meaning and value, and in believing that the sciences or philosophies can themselves be other than "conventional and qualified by the nature of the animal psyches in which they are evoked."[6]

Although in one respect Santayana obviously had great confidence in science, in another it is clear that he trusted scientific perspectives and ideas even less than he trusted the arts and religions. Certainly he was not altogether averse to appealing to the authority of science in the defense of materialism. His materialism, however, unlike that of many nineteenth-century scientists and philosophers, was not inspired primarily by science. Though he thought modern physics supported it, his materialism was essentially that of Lucretius: unscientific, aesthetic, and moral, a sense that dark, impersonal, and indifferent powers determine every event. This view as such, he thought, can inspire neither love nor fear; but it can for this very reason provide, in the words of Lucretius, "the lofty and serene positions well fortified by the learning of the wise, from which [one] may look down upon others and see them wandering all abroad and going astray in their search for the path of life. . . ."[7] Thus materialism justifies intellectual detachment; but it also makes illusion inevitable. For since matter itself is never known, the materialist must claim that in the analysis of knowledge, "Nothing is ultimately left except the passing appearance or the appearance of something passing."[8] Of course the phenomenologist, Edmund Husserl, made a very similar claim, though he assumed that the structure of appearance will finally reveal the structure of existence. Santayana, however, not only had no such faith in appearance but also doubted, as already noted, that structure or so-called law signified anything conclusive about the actual character of existence. Thus he might have said with Ludwig Wittgenstein that "At the basis of the whole modern view of the world lies the illusion that the so-called laws of nature are the explanations of natural phenomena."[9] What he did in fact say was that science is "tentative, genial, practical, and humane, full of ideality and pathos, like every great human undertaking."[10] But science, like religion, is by no means rendered completely meaningless or futile by the illusions it generates or represents. Science is "useful and delightful," he said, though it is also "essentially fallible" and, like all knowledge, "only a claim put forth, a part of that unfathomable compulsion by force of which we live and hold our painted world together for a moment."[11] So he could never have added, as Wittgenstein did, that "The proposition is a picture of reality" and "The logical propositions describe the scaffolding or rather they present it."[12] The "painted world" of Santayana is purely fictional or imaginative and illusory through and through, even though it may be pragmatically or experimentally verified. Thus Wittgenstein's view of science is finally quite different from that of Santayana; for he still reflected faith in an ideal of logical coherence and clarity that leads ultimately to reality; but Santayana's view is based on the assumption that disillusion is the only wisdom in an opaque and intractable world.

More than most men, it has been claimed, Santayana apparently had a profound sense of being carried along by the current of events without in any measure affecting those events. Evidently his view of science, as well as his philosophy of religion and morals, was intimately related to this sense of being in the grip of "some alien and inscrutable power"—of living, thinking, and dying without the power to live or think or die. Therefore all "human experience and science are spiritual responses in an animal to a material world quite beyond their jurisdiction, but controlling their development."[13] Man as scientist no less than man as poet or saint is thus ultimately dependent on powers that work in and through him; he knows only his own reactions to existence and not existence itself. For "the animality of the mind"[14] means among other things that science, "in so far as it is a calculus applicable to crude facts, may figure among those picturesque popular beliefs which I call knowledge of existence, not because they are not symbolic in texture and essentially fantastic, but because being so they are truly symbolic in intent and function."[15] Science, along with other forms of knowledge, is only "a justified illusion, an irrational pretension by chance fulfilled, a chance shot hitting the mark."[16]

"To live by science," Santayana said, "requires intelligence and faith, but not to live by it is folly."[17] Yet he was also clearly convinced that the needs and hopes of man will never in fact be satisfied or fulfilled by science. "Knowledge of the world and of what is possible in it, though it may discourage some vice," he wrote, "will not solve for us the question of what is our true good. For what the world can offer, when tried, may seem to us vanity."[18] Not to live by science is folly then only because science may provide the basis of health and security that are in turn the foundation of sanity in morals and all the spiritual goods that are possible. Ultimately, however, science, he thought, can neither discover the truth—though it may catch a glimpse of it in its own special modes—nor guide man to a fulfillment of his hopes and needs. The claims and promises of the sciences are no less illusory—and no less in need of purification by disillusion—than the claims of the various religions. All orthodoxy apparently, whether in religion, morals, or science, "must be taken with a grain of salt, to keep it beneficent and prevent it from turning into madness."[19]

What about philosophy? There can be no doubt that Santayana regarded most if not all philosophy as also tentative, imaginative, "a painted world," and therefore no less illusory than religion or science. "At heart," he wrote, "these finer philosophers [Bergson and Hegel in particular], like Plato, are not seeking to describe the world of our daily plodding and commerce, but to supply a visionary interpretation of it, a refuge from it in some contrasted spiritual assurance, where the sharp facts vanish into a clarified drama or a pleasant trance."[20] That he sometimes denied the truth of his own philosophical distinctions and perspective has already been noted. His own philosophy, he said, aspired "to be only a contribution to the humanities, the expression of a reflective, selective, and free mind."[21] He also expressed the same point by saying that he "set out to describe, not nature or God, but the ideas of God or nature bred in the human mind."[22] And even this task, he recognized, always involves imaginative sympathy and presumption. So the achievement of the philosopher, he thought, will always be both more and less than the truth; for he "may raise a monument as vast as he will; it will be his prison while he lives, and his tomb afterwards. He may paint its walls with a panorama of the universe, but he cannot include himself painting it—except perhaps in a playful episode in one corner: and then that miniature will not be at all the inclusive enacted event, the actual episode in the life of nature, which contained himself, his monument, his model, and his painting."[23] But he also said that although the imaginative, poetic, and dialectical values may be genuine and important, "after all it is a great advantage for a system of philosophy to be substantially true."[24]

Substantially true? What can this mean in a philosophy that also claimed that "nothing given exists" and that the "scientific world" as well as poetry, religion, and philosophy are all equally and inevitably products of imagination and art? Santayana had no doubt that the world has (as C. S. Peirce put it) a real character (the truth) that is independent of what anyone happens to think or believe about it; but unlike Peirce he was not convinced that inquiry, if carried far enough, is fated to discover the actual character of things. Instead, he obviously thought, every appearance and every model or theory must misrepresent to a greater or lesser extent the totality, character, and relations of facts. "Every part of experience, as it comes, is illusion; and the source of this illusion is my animal nature, blindly labouring in a blind world."[25] If this is so, surely the only "substantially true" philosophy can be none other than one that recognizes the "inevitable illusion" infecting every version of experience and thought. Experience and the claims and systems based on it may provide relatively reliable guides to conduct, to future appearances and relations. To that degree they may be trusted—or indeed *must* be trusted. But to claim that current sciences or philosophies are more than this, or to suppose that they will never be replaced by utterly different and yet equally or more reliable systems and claims, is, he thought, wholly unjustified. He believed apparently that the only certain truth is that no matter what the forms of experience or the modes of inquiry and interpretation, all these will prove illusory and men will be their victims except insofar as they recognize illusion as their inescapable fate.

Consequently Santayana denied that his own philosophy was true in any radical sense and claimed only that it reexpressed from his own point of view "the conventional truths" adopted by those in the West who have sought to live in the spirit. His only distinction, he thought, was that he recognized the arbitrary and illusory elements in his choices and claims. The possession of certain or absolute truth, he said, is beyond the range of the human mind. Indeed he often emphasized that the basic task of the philosopher is not to discover the truth. "The business of a philosopher is rather to be a good shepherd of his thoughts. . . . He will do well to endow his vision of things with all the force, colour, and scope of which his soul is capable. Then if he misses the truth of nature, as in many things is probable, he will at least have achieved a work of imagination."[26] The philosopher, then, like the poet and the scientist, never discovers the world as it is but only creates more or less reliable models and perspectives in thought. He can know the truth, if at all, only insofar as he discounts the illusion that is the inevitable result of a complex world and his own perplexing life in it.

Perhaps the chief wisdom of Santayana was that he granted a kind of equality to all the various forms of experience and judgment. If he finally disparaged and distrusted one spiritual and judicial form, he disparaged and distrusted all. Unlike so many who have sought to discredit science for the sake of religion or religion for the sake of science, he established no hierarchy of methods; he believed that all the ways in which man interprets or orients himself to the world, though not without unavoidable illusions, may be nonetheless both functionally reliable and intrinsically splendid. Few men have loved the arts and religions more than he did, and few have been more willing to leave "the last word" about "existence" to the scientists without thereby abdicating his own intellect or becoming credulous in the face of problems and methods he did not pretend to understand. So if he thought that the ultimate and necessary result of every method of inquiry and judgment is illusion, there was at least some similarity to the humble words of Socrates in *The Phaedo:* "A man of sense will not insist that these things are exactly as I have described them. But I think that he will believe that something of this kind is true. . . ." Of course he did not share in the least the Socratic faith that the order of existence is finally, if mysteriously, beneficent. Instead he sought to nourish and protect the human spirit in a world in which, as he understood it, "The last word must always be a contradiction of our ideals, of those ideals which alone make things good or bad. The world becomes one oppressive, tyrannous fact, eternally and inexplicably present."[27]

Beginning with the assumption that matter (or blind impersonal and indifferent fertility) is the basic existential fact on which all other facts and appearances are utterly dependent, Santayana had no choice except to regard religion, the arts, science, and philosophy as essentially symbolic—or more accurately, as merely symptomatic—of the dark and impenetrable source and sustainer of life and light. "The light of the spirit which shines in the darkness cannot see the primeval darkness which begat it and which it dispels."[28] Ideas, images, sounds, and words, if they signify anything at all, cannot be more than the ephemeral results of an existential nexus that is in itself utterly different from both the signs and the appearances that are their specious objects. "The appearances are not parts of the material objects, since they change with the distance, position, and condition of the observer."[29] Yet only appearances can be known. The import of the claim that all knowledge is symbolic is clear: man's acquaintance with himself and the world is at best superficial, only provisionally validated, and extremely limited. One cannot be logically or even morally certain of anything except his own convictions and judgments. Dogmatism is completely unjustified. Indeed the world may be confidently judged religiously and artistically or scientifically and philosophically only if proper precautions are first taken against illusion. The dark fertility of nature is unfathomed and unaffected by the visions and revisions stimulated in the minds of men. He was not then merely rhetorical in the early sonnet which ended: "Truth is a dream, unless my dream is true."[30] Later, in order to deny emphatically that dreams are true, he insisted that it is only by animal faith—by an instinctive and unquestioning belief in the externality of the objects of perception or judgment—that any view or claim may be judged true or false. "Truth was therefore—not really a dream in itself, since no mind was ever to see it—but something which it was a vain dream to look for, or to think we possessed in our philosophy."[31]

In spite of the paradox involved, the candid and honest mind cannot easily dismiss the claim that human experience and judgment are endemically illusory. There is too much evidence that supports it. Yet evidently most men, being dogmatists by predilection as well as by practical necessity, come only slowly and often too late, if at all, to question the reliability of their own claims or to admit the possibly greater relevance and validity of the contrary claims of others. But apparently Santayana was congenitally a sceptic. He thought no form of judgment, no claim or experience, really trustworthy. There is surely a scrupulous honesty in such doubt, and the cheerful sceptic is always a welcome relief amongst a herd of earnest dogmatists. But if dogmatism is unjustified and unnecessary, or if all knowledge is more or less—or even radically—tentative, there are nonetheless utterly sane and inescapable reasons for regarding science and philosophy, and in some important respects the arts and religions as well, as modes of genuine discovery or veridical judgment. Apart from the question of the kind of world that would result from widespread adoption of the view that no form of experience or judgment is trustworthy, and apart from the paradox involved in making such claims, there can be no honest escape from the necessity of supposing that judgment, carefully and candidly rendered, may reveal at least partially the character of existence without radical distortion or illusion. For after all the world that man knows best is in many respects a product of his own effort, judgment, and knowledge—products of his labor, his art, his worship, and his patient inquiries—and is surely the most substantial of illusions if indeed illusion at all.

Santayana's own works are in fact parts of that world, parts that, contrary to his own claims, apparently enter into the existential order and become, at least for a time, an influence on the thoughts and decisions of other men. Nothing seems more certain of course than that scientific innovation and discovery will continue or that the arts, religions, and philosophy will continually undergo revolutions as long as man's spirit endures and his intellect remains viable. But does this necessarily mean that such enterprises are altogether imaginative and do not reveal at all the character of existence? A positive reply to this question is really indefensible. Plato, who maintained that the real is the knowable, and Aristotle, who insisted that the mind can indeed know things as they are because its only characteristic is pure potentiality—or the power to become whatever it knows—may have overestimated the affinity between the mind and its objects or the congruity between existence and knowledge of existence. Nonetheless the world that man inhabits is in very important respects a human world—regardless of the nature of its origins. And man knows the world in certain respects simply by being intimately and inextricably a part of it. So long as his experience and choice maintain the direction of life and inquiry, and so long as his methods of judgment continue to disclose dimensions and features that were formerly hidden or to make existence richer with new creations, it seems altogether pointless to claim seriously that he is the victim of illusion. A logic that simply keeps men reasonable and their dialogue mutually intelligible surely reveals a part of the world no less truly than a logic that reflects the structure of a thoroughly rational and predictable world. And if man must finally trust his logic in order to remain reasonable and intelligible to others, then surely he may also trust his moral judgments, his sciences, his arts, and his religions for similar, if somewhat less obvious, reasons. For by judging the world morally, the world may be kept moral; through scientific inquiries the sciences may become a more pervasive and beneficent part of the world; and the explorations and products of the religions and the arts may, respectively and together, keep the world holy and aesthetically profound and pleasing. To claim that ideas or systems of thought are illusory unless they do more than this is in effect to refuse to identify as knowledge anything short of omniscience and absolute certainty.

Santayana's affections and sensitivities were apparently such that he found it terribly difficult or impossible to accept less than perfection in any object or activity. So if knowledge and hope could not be perfect, illusion and despair must become the final standard of all judgment! Yet if, as suggested above, each form of experience and each discipline is in some measure creative, inventing and sustaining the conditions of its reliability and truth instead of merely reflecting or pointing to a completely independent reality, his work was not without great value. He himself did much, not to increase illusions that must be discounted, but to encourage sensitivities and perspectives that may help to keep the world both philosophical and beautiful. For the disillusion he found morally and intellectually defensible was, at least for the most part, not the disillusion of ignorance forbidden to eat the fruit of the tree of knowledge but the disillusion of wisdom provoked that wisdom does not altogether rule the world. He was himself, if his own terms may be used, an extraordinary instance of universal "Spirit . . . this ever-renewed witness . . . and judge of existence, divine yet born of woman."[32] If he uncharitably described himself as a victim as well as a fascinated witness of existence, he may nonetheless be judged also by his own standards of charity. And "charity will always judge a soul," he said, "not by what it has succeeded in fashioning externally, not by the body or the words or the works that are the wreckage of its voyage, but by the elements of light and love that this soul infused into that inevitable tragedy."[33] By this standard George Santayana was not only a philosopher but a man whose clear and intense affections united him in aspiration with all the perfections that the world so often suggests but all too rarely achieves.

NOTES

Chapter 1

1. *Character and Opinion in the United States, with Reminiscences of William James and Josiah Royce and Academic Life in America,* p. v.
2. *Classic American Philosophers,* Max H. Fisch (ed.), in "Introduction to Santayana," by Philip B. Rice, p. 257.
3. "Apologia Pro Mente Sua," *The Philosophy of George Santayana,* Paul Arthur Schlipp (ed.), pp. 601–602.
4. *Ibid.,* p. 603.
5. John E. Smith, *The Spirit of American Philosophy,* p. xiv.
6. *Realms of Being,* p. 827.
7. *The Letters of George Santayana,* p. 28.
8. John Dewey, *Essays in Experimental Logic,* p. 306.
9. *Realms of Being,* p. 827.
10. *Ibid.,* p. 561.
11. John Dewey, *Logic,* p. 70.
12. *Realms of Being,* p. 835.
13. *Ibid.,* p. 841.
14. *Ibid.,* p. 833.
15. *Persons and Places,* p. 240.
16. *Three Philosophical Poets,* p. 206.

Chapter 2

1. "A General Confession," *The Philosophy of George Santayana,* Paul Arthur Schlipp (ed.), p. 3.
2. *Persons and Places,* p. 138.
3. *Soliloquies in England and Later Soliloquies,* p. 3.
4. Baker Brownell, "Santayana, the Man and the Philosopher," *The Philosophy of George Santayana,* Paul Arthur Schlipp (ed.), p. 53.
5. *Persons and Places,* p. 140.
6. *Ibid.,* p. 20.

7. *Ibid.*, p. 178.
8. *Ibid.*, p. 85.
9. *Ibid.*, p. 114.
10. *Ibid.*, pp. 114–115.
11. *Ibid.*, pp. 164–165.
12. *Ibid.*, p. 162.
13. *Ibid.*, p. 238.
14. *Ibid.*, p. 203.
15. *Ibid.*, p. 221.
16. *Ibid.*, p. 239.
17. *Ibid.*, p. 241.
18. "Sonnet III."
19. *The Middle Span,* p. 177.
20. *Persons and Places,* p. 241.
21. *Ibid.*, p. 249.
22. *The Middle Span,* pp. 1–2.
23. *Ibid.*, pp. 6–7.
24. *Ibid.*, p. 10.
25. *Ibid.*, p. 9.
26. "Apologia Pro Mente Sua," *The Philosophy of George Santayana,* Paul Arthur Schlipp (ed.), p. 601.
27. *The Idler and His Works,* p. 11.
28. "A General Confession," *The Philosophy of George Santayana,* Paul Arthur Schlipp (ed.), p. 13.
29. *My Host the World,* p. 11.
30. *Ibid.*, p. 8.
31. *Ibid.*, p. 109.
32. "To W.P., II."
33. "To W.P., III."
34. "To W.P., IV."
35. *My Host the World,* p. 8.
36. *Ibid.*, p. 9.
37. *Persons and Places,* p. 75.
38. *Ibid.*, p. 87.
39. *Ibid.*, p. 84.
40. *My Host the World,* p. 4.
41. *Persons and Places,* p. 92.
42. *My Host the World,* p. 10.
43. *Persons and Places,* p. 79.
44. *My Host the World,* p. 11.
45. Dylan Thomas, "Poem in October," in *The Collected Poems of Dylan Thomas,* p. 115.
46. *My Host the World,* p. 11.
47. *Ibid.*, p. 13.

48. *Ibid.,* p. 14.
49. "Sonnet L."
50. *My Host the World,* p. 25.
51. *Ibid.,* pp. 25–26.
52. Baker Brownell, "Santayana, the Man and the Philosopher," *The Philosophy of George Santayana,* Paul Arthur Schlipp (ed.), p. 48.
53. *American Mercury,* Vol. I, 1924, p. 69.
54. Baker Brownell, "Santayana, the Man and the Philosopher," *The Philosophy of George Santayana,* Paul Arthur Schlipp (ed.), p. 35.
55. *Soliloquies in England and Later Soliloquies,* p. 184.
56. *Winds of Doctrine,* p. 146.
57. *My Host the World,* p. 32.
58. *Persons and Places,* p. 88.
59. *The Middle Span,* p. 110.
60. *My Host the World,* p. 2.
61. *The Middle Span,* pp. 35–36.
62. *My Host the World,* pp. 134–135.
63. *The Moral Philosophy of Santayana,* edited with foreword by Irwin Edman, p. lxii.
64. "Apologia Pro Mente Sua," *The Philosophy of George Santayana,* Paul Arthur Schlipp (ed.), p. 571.
65. *The Middle Span,* p. 10.
66. *Ibid.,* p. 159.
67. *Ibid.,* p. 166.
68. *Ibid.,* p. 181.
69. *Ibid.,* p. 181.
70. *Ibid.,* p. 181.
71. *My Host the World,* p. 96.
72. *Ibid.,* p. 100.
73. *The Idler and His Works,* p. 20.
74. *Dominations and Powers,* p. 22.
75. *My Host the World,* p. 139.
76. *The Letters of George Santayana,* p. 357.
77. *The Poet's Testament,* p. 14.

Chapter 3

1. Josiah Royce, *The World and the Individual,* Vol. I, p. 327.
2. *Realms of Being,* p. 549.

3. *Ibid.*, pp. 549–550.
4. Charles S. Peirce, *Philosophical Writings of Peirce,* Justus Buchler (ed.), p. 322.
5. William James, *Essays in Radical Empiricism,* p. 25.
6. John Dewey, *Experience, Nature, and Freedom,* p. 47.
7. John Dewey, *Experience and Nature,* p. 258.
8. *Ibid.*, p. 307.
9. *Scepticism and Animal Faith,* p. 286.
10. *Obiter Scripta,* p. 284.
11. G. E. Moore, *Philosophical Studies,* p. 17.
12. *Scepticism and Animal Faith,* p. 272.
13. *Soliloquies in England and Later Soliloquies,* p. 2.
14. *Ibid.*, p. 225.
15. *Realms of Being,* p. 573.
16. *Soliloquies in England and Later Soliloquies,* p. 219.
17. *Realms of Being,* p. 388.
18. William James, *The Principles of Psychology,* p. 146.
19. *Ibid.*, p. 149.
20. "Apologia Pro Mente Sua," *The Philosophy of George Santayana,* Paul Arthur Schlipp (ed.), p. 508.
21. *Ibid.*, p. 504.
22. *Ibid.*, pp. 507–508.
23. "A General Confession," *The Philosophy of George Santayana,* Paul Arthur Schlipp (ed.), p. 18.
24. "Apologia Pro Mente Sua," *The Philosophy of George Santayana,* Paul Arthur Schlipp (ed.), p. 600.
25. *Soliloquies in England and Later Soliloquies,* pp. 219–220.
26. *The Middle Span,* p. 8.
27. *The Idler and His Works,* p. 18.
28. *Realms of Being,* pp. 564–565.
29. *Ibid.*, p. 390.
30. *Ibid.*, p. 234.
31. *Dominations and Powers,* p. 18; *The Idler and His Works,* p. 51.
32. *The Idler and His Works,* pp. 35–36.
33. *Realms of Being,* p. 558.

Chapter 4

1. *Realms of Being,* p. 5.
2. *Ibid.*, p. viii.
3. *Ibid.*, p. 156.

4. William James, *A Pluralistic Universe,* p. 212.
5. *Scepticism and Animal Faith,* p. 48.
6. *Ibid.,* p. 185.
7. *Soliloquies in England and Later Soliloquies,* p. 2.
8. *The Letters of George Santayana,* p. 330.
9. *Scepticism and Animal Faith,* p. 185.
10. *Ibid.,* Chapter VII.
11. *Ibid.,* p. 45.
12. *Ibid.,* pp. 45–46.
13. *Ibid.,* p. 47.
14. *Realms of Being,* p. 156.
15. *Ibid.,* pp. 160–164.
16. *Ibid.,* p. 170.
17. *Ibid.,* p. 171.
18. This feature of Whitehead's thought was first pointed out to me by my good friend, David Smillie, of the Department of Psychology at Duquesne University.
19. *Scepticism and Animal Faith,* p. 48.
20. Edmund Husserl, *Ideas: General Introduction to a Pure Phenomenology,* p. 44.
21. *Realms of Being,* pp. 172–174.
22. Charles S. Peirce, *Values in a Universe of Chance,* Philip Weiner (ed.), p. 130.
23. Charles S. Peirce, *Philosophical Writings of Peirce,* Justus Buchler (ed.), p. 74.
24. *Ibid.,* pp. 76–78.
25. *Ibid.,* p. 76.
26. *Realms of Being,* p. 5.
27. Charles S. Peirce, *Philosophical Writings of Peirce,* Justus Buchler (ed.), p. 76.
28. *Realms of Being,* p. 27.
29. *Ibid.,* p. 27.
30. Notes made by Baker Brownell on W. Arnett's *Santayana and the Sense of Beauty.*
31. Charles S. Peirce, *Philosophical Writings of Peirce,* Justus Buchler (ed.), p. 77.
32. *Realms of Being,* p. 189.
33. Charles S. Peirce, *Philosophical Writings of Peirce,* Justus Buchler (ed.), p. 78.
34. *Ibid.,* pp. 92–93.
35. *Ibid.,* p. 78.
36. *Realms of Being,* p. viii.
37. John Dewey, *Experience and Nature,* pp. 287–288.

Chapter 5

1. *The Sense of Beauty,* p. 191.
2. "A General Confession," *The Philosophy of George Santayana,* Paul Arthur Schlipp (ed.), p. 7.
3. *Persons and Places,* p. 172.
4. *Realms of Being,* pp. 418–419.
5. *Ibid.,* p. xi.
6. *Scepticism and Animal Faith,* p. 181.
7. Josiah Royce, *The Problem of Christianity,* Vol. II, p. 323.
8. Josiah Royce, *The World and the Individual,* Vol. I, p. 309.
9. *Ibid.,* p. 36.
10. Charles S. Peirce, "The Fixation of Belief," *Classic American Philosophers,* Max H. Fisch (ed.), in a footnote on p. 61.
11. William James, *Pragmatism: A New Name for Some Old Ways of Thinking,* p. 218.
12. *Reason in Science,* p. 32.
13. *Realms of Being,* p. 449.
14. *Ibid.,* p. 448.
15. "A General Confession," *The Philosophy of George Santayana,* Paul Arthur Schlipp (ed.), p. 14.
16. John Dewey, *Essays in Experimental Logic,* pp. 24–25.
17. *Realms of Being,* p. 420.
18. *Soliloquies in England and Later Soliloquies,* pp. 122–123.
19. *Scepticism and Animal Faith,* p. 179.
20. *Ibid.,* p. 164.
21. *Reason in Common Sense,* p. 15.
22. *Realms of Being,* p. 469.
23. *Scepticism and Animal Faith,* p. 179.
24. *Ibid.,* p. 16.
25. *Realms of Being,* p. 456.
26. *Ibid.,* p. 829.
27. William James, *Pragmatism: A New Name for Some Old Ways of Thinking,* p. 213.
28. *Realms of Being,* p. 830.
29. *Reason in Religion,* p. 10.
30. *Ibid.,* p. 14.
31. *Ibid.,* p. 11.

32. *Obiter Scripta,* p. 224.
33. *Realms of Being,* p. 540.
34. *Ibid.,* p. 546.
35. *Ibid.,* p. xiii.
36. *Ibid.,* p. xxxii.
37. *Ibid.,* p. xxxii.
38. *Scepticism and Animal Faith,* pp. 72–73.
39. *Ibid.,* pp. 17–18.

Chapter 6

1. *Realms of Being,* pp. 311–312.
2. *Dominations and Powers,* pp. 52–53.
3. J. S. Mill, *A System of Logic,* Fifth Edition, pp. 385–386.
4. Chauncey Wright, *Philosophical Writings of Chauncey Wright,* Edward H. Madden (ed.), pp. 36–37.
5. Charles S. Peirce, "The Doctrine of Necessity Examined," *Philosophical Writings of Peirce,* Justus Buchler (ed.), pp. 324–338.
6. *Realms of Being,* p. 274.
7. William James, *The Will To Believe and Other Essays in Popular Philosophy,* pp. 167ff.
8. Charles S. Peirce, *Philosophical Writings of Peirce,* Justus Buchler (ed.), p. 337.
9. *Scepticism and Animal Faith,* p. 236.
10. John Dewey, *Experience, Nature, and Freedom,* p. 267.
11. *Ibid.,* p. 275.
12. John Dewey, *Experience and Nature,* p. 42.
13. *Ibid.,* p. 47.
14. *Ibid.,* p. 76.
15. John Dewey, *A Common Faith,* p. 24.
16. *Obiter Scripta,* pp. 226–227.
17. *Ibid.,* p. 233.
18. *The Letters of George Santayana,* p. 372.
19. *Lotze's System of Philosophy,* p. 86.
20. *Scepticism and Animal Faith,* p. 186.
21. *The Idea of Christ in the Gospels,* p. 253.
22. *Ibid.,* p. 192.
23. *Scepticism and Animal Faith,* p. 285.
24. *Realms of Being,* p. 80.
25. *Ibid.,* p. 388.
26. *Ibid.,* p. 291.

27. *Scepticism and Animal Faith,* p. 236.
28. *Persons and Places,* p. 2.
29. *Realms of Being,* p. 313.
30. *Ibid.,* p. 320.
31. *Ibid.,* p. 628.
32. *Ibid.,* pp. 628–629.
33. *Ibid.,* p. 319.
34. *Ibid.,* p. 310.
35. *Ibid.,* p. 323.
36. *Ibid.,* p. 386.
37. *Ibid.,* p. 319.
38. *Ibid.,* p. 319.
39. *Ibid.,* p. 326.
40. *Reason in Science,* pp. 76–78.
41. *The Idler and His Works,* pp. 3–4.

Chapter 7

1. *Reason in Religion,* p. 27.
2. *Ibid.,* p. 31.
3. *Ibid.,* p. 30.
4. *Ibid.,* pp. 141–143.
5. *Ibid.,* p. 158.
6. *Ibid.,* p. 156.
7. *Ibid.,* p. 137.
8. *Dominations and Powers,* p. 19.
9. *The Idea of Christ in the Gospels,* p. 252.
10. *Realms of Being,* p. 397.
11. *Egotism in German Philosophy,* p. 154.
12. *Realms of Being,* pp. 413–414.
13. *Ibid.,* p. 415.
14. *Ibid.,* p. 416.
15. *Ibid.,* pp. 838–839.
16. *Lotze's System of Philosophy,* p. 87.
17. *Scepticism and Animal Faith,* p. 130.
18. *Reason in Religion,* p. 130.
19. *Scepticism and Animal Faith,* pp. 177–178.
20. *Ibid.,* pp. 11–12.
21. *Reason in Religion,* pp. 10–11.
22. *Reason in Common Sense,* p. 144.
23. *Reason in Religion,* pp. 11–12.
24. *Ibid.,* p. 12.
25. *The Middle Span,* p. 20.

26. *Reason in Religion,* p. 275.
27. *Dominations and Powers,* p. 21.
28. *Ibid.,* p. 160.
29. *Interpretations of Poetry and Religion,* p. 6.
30. *Dominations and Powers,* p. 291.
31. *Reason in Religion,* p. 275.
32. *Dominations and Powers,* pp. 155–156.
33. *Ibid.,* pp. 158–159.
34. *Character and Opinion in the United States,* p. 233.
35. Charles S. Peirce, *Values in a Universe of Chance,* Philip Weiner (ed.), p. 365.
36. William James, *The Will To Believe,* p. 51.
37. *Soliloquies in England and Later Soliloquies,* p. 247.
38. *Interpretations of Poetry and Religion,* p. 289.
39. John Dewey, *A Common Faith,* pp. 42–43.
40. *The Idler and His Works,* p. 165.
41. *Ibid.,* p. 177.
42. *Reason in Society,* p. 201.
43. *Reason in Religion,* p. 43.
44. *Realms of Being,* p. 801.
45. *Ibid.,* p. 798.
46. *Winds of Doctrine,* p. 50.
47. *Ibid.,* p. 56.
48. "Sonnet IV."
49. *Dominations and Powers,* p. 302.

Chapter 8

1. *Reason in Science,* pp. 214–215.
2. *Realms of Being,* p. 483.
3. *Ibid.,* p. 332.
4. *Ibid.,* p. 482.
5. *Ibid.,* p. 478.
6. *Dominations and Powers,* p. 4.
7. *Ibid.,* p. 2.
8. *Realms of Being,* p. 479.
9. *Reason in Science,* p. 217.
10. *Realms of Being,* p. 483.
11. *Reason in Science,* p. 216.
12. *Obiter Scripta,* p. 88.
13. *Ibid.,* p. 93.
14. *Ibid.,* p. 71.

15. *Ibid.*, p. 72.
16. Bertrand Russell, "The Elements of Ethics," cited in *Winds of Doctrine*, pp. 140–141.
17. *Winds of Doctrine*, p. 141.
18. *Ibid.*, p. 144.
19. *Ibid.*, p. 149.
20. *Dominations and Powers*, p. 63.
21. *Reason in Science*, p. 211.
22. "Apologia Pro Mente Sua," *The Philosophy of George Santayana*, Paul Arthur Schlipp (ed.), p. 563.
23. *Reason in Science*, p. 249.
24. *Dialogues in Limbo*, p. 123.
25. *Reason in Science*, p. 254.
26. *Reason in Common Sense*, p. 238.
27. *Reason in Science*, pp. 252–253.
28. *Ibid.*, p. 263.
29. *Ibid.*, p. 266.
30. *Ibid.*, p. 267.
31. *Ibid.*, p. 295.
32. *Ibid.*, p. 300.
33. *Realms of Being*, p. 475.
34. *Ibid.*, pp. 479–480.
35. *Ibid.*, p. 474.
36. *Winds of Doctrine*, p. 151.
37. *Realms of Being*, p. 683.
38. William James, "The Moral Philosopher and the Moral Life," *The Will To Believe*, pp. 184–215.
39. John Dewey, *Experience and Nature*, p. 424.
40. *Dominations and Powers*, p. vii.
41. *Reason in Society*, p. 112.
42. *Dominations and Powers*, pp. 109–110.
43. *Ibid.*, pp. 348–349.
44. *Ibid.*, p. 351.
45. *Ibid.*, p. 358.
46. *Ibid.*, p. 353.
47. *Ibid.*, p. 430.
48. *Ibid.*, pp. 422–424.
49. *Ibid.*, p. 402.
50. *Reason in Society*, p. 128.
51. *Ibid.*, pp. 129–130.
52. *Ibid.*, p. 121.
53. *Ibid.*, p. 127.
54. *Dominations and Powers*, pp. 462–463.
55. *Ibid.*, p. 358.

Chapter 9

1. *The Sense of Beauty,* p. v.
2. *Dominations and Powers,* p. ix.
3. *Reason in Art,* pp. 174–175.
4. *Realms of Being,* p. xi.
5. *Reason in Art,* pp. 229–230.
6. *The Sense of Beauty,* p. 270.
7. *Reason in Art,* p. 13.
8. *Dominations and Powers,* p. 16.
9. *Reason in Art,* pp. 16–17.
10. *Scepticism and Animal Faith,* pp. 102–103.
11. *Reason in Art,* p. 13.
12. *Three Philosophical Poets,* pp. 212–214.
13. *Reason in Art,* p. 130.
14. *Ibid.,* p. 152.
15. *Ibid.,* p. 85.
16. *Ibid.,* p. 209.
17. *Obiter Scripta,* pp. 251–252.
18. *Ibid.,* p. 251.
19. *Ibid.,* pp. 259–261.
20. *Dominations and Powers,* p. 277.
21. *Reason in Art,* p. 129.
22. *Interpretations of Poetry and Religion,* p. 19.
23. *The Sense of Beauty,* p. 29.
24. *Ibid.,* p. 11.
25. *Soliloquies in England and Later Soliloquies,* p. 254.
26. *Dominations and Powers,* p. ix.
27. *Reason in Art,* p. 135.
28. *Ibid.,* p. 149.
29. *Ibid.,* p. 161.
30. *Ibid.,* p. 84.
31. *Ibid.,* p. 39.
32. *Ibid.,* pp. 54–57.
33. *Ibid.,* p. 112.
34. *Ibid.,* pp. 114–115.
35. *Ibid.,* pp. 117–118.
36. *Realms of Being,* p. 153.
37. *Reason in Art,* p. 122.
38. *Ibid.,* p. 167.
39. *The Sense of Beauty,* p. 27.
40. *Reason in Art,* p. 179.

41. *Ibid.*, pp. 172–174.
42. *Ibid.*, p. 180.
43. *Ibid.*, pp. 188–189.
44. *Ibid.*, p. 188.
45. "A General Confession," *The Philosophy of George Santayana*, Paul Arthur Schlipp (ed.), p. 21.
46. *Reason in Art*, pp. 177–178.
47. *Ibid.*, pp. 195–196.
48. *Ibid.*, pp. 203–204.
49. *Ibid.*, p. 207.
50. *Dominations and Powers*, p. viii.
51. *Obiter Scripta*, p. 37.
52. *Reason in Art*, p. 190.
53. *Ibid.*, p. 215.
54. *Ibid.*, p. 66.
55. John Dewey, *Experience and Nature*, p. 378.
56. *Ibid.*, p. 363.
57. *Ibid.*, p. 359.
58. *Ibid.*, p. 364.
59. John Dewey, *Art as Experience*, p. 8.
60. John Dewey, *Experience and Nature*, p. 389.

Chapter 10

1. *Scepticism and Animal Faith*, pp. 72–73.
2. *My Host the World*, p. 32.
3. *Ibid.*, p. 4.
4. *The Idler and His Works*, p. 25.
5. *Ibid.*, p. 15.
6. "Apologia Pro Mente Sua," *The Philosophy of George Santayana*, Paul Arthur Schlipp (ed.), p. 508.
7. Lucretius, *On the Nature of Things*, Book II.
8. *Realms of Being*, p. 200.
9. Ludwig Wittgenstein, *Tractatus Logico-Philosophicus*, 6.371.
10. *Reason in Science*, p. 309.
11. *Ibid.*, p. 318.
12. Ludwig Wittgenstein, *Tractatus Logico-Philosophicus*, 4.01; 6.371.
13. *The Idler and His Works*, p. 130.
14. "Apologia Pro Mente Sua," *The Philosophy of George Santayana*, Paul Arthur Schlipp (ed.), p. 601.
15. *The Idler and His Works*, p. 133.

16. *Reason in Common Sense,* p. 151.
17. *Reason in Science,* p. 319.
18. *Dominations and Powers,* p. 465.
19. *Persons and Places,* p. 92.
20. *Obiter Scripta,* p. 163.
21. *The Middle Span,* p. 156.
22. "A General Confession," *The Philosophy of George Santayana,* Paul Arthur Schlipp (ed.), p. 15.
23. *The Idler and His Works,* p. 127.
24. *Obiter Scripta,* p. 163.
25. *Scepticism and Animal Faith,* p. 52.
26. *Realms of Being,* pp. xv–xvi.
27. *The Idler and His Works,* p. 86.
28. *Realms of Being,* p. 249.
29. *Dominations and Powers,* p. 19.
30. "Sonnet V."
31. *My Host the World,* p. 32.
32. *Ibid.,* p. 144.
33. *Persons and Places,* p. 95.

ANNOTATED BIBLIOGRAPHY OF THE CHIEF PHILOSOPHICAL WORKS OF GEORGE SANTAYANA

Lotze's System of Philosophy. Dissertation submitted in 1889 for the degree, Doctor of Philosophy, Harvard University. An examination of the idealism of Rudolf Hermann Lotze (1817–1881). Discusses Lotze's relation to Kant, to natural science, his view of causality, theism, and aesthetics. Professor Paul Kuntz is preparing an edition for publication.

The Sense of Beauty: Being the Outlines of Aesthetic Theory. New York: Charles Scribner's Sons, 1896. Several editions are now available. Concerned basically with "the theory and history of aesthetics." The central themes are the nature, the materials, and the formal elements of beauty together with a theory of the ways in which the arts achieve expression.

Interpretations of Poetry and Religion. New York: Charles Scribner's Sons, 1900. Now available in a Harper Torchbook. Besides discussion of the Homeric hymns, Shakespeare, Whitman, Browning, and Emerson, this book contains the first and perhaps clearest statement of the claim that poetry and religion are essentially identical.

Reason in Common Sense, Volume I of *The Life of Reason or The Phases of Human Progress.* New York: Charles Scribner's Sons, 1905. Defines the scope of the five volumes and develops concepts of reason, mind, and the relations of things and ideas. This and the following four volumes are available in paperback Collier Books.

Reason in Society, Volume II of *The Life of Reason.* New York: Charles Scribner's Sons, 1905. Discusses the basis, the forms, and the ideals presumably implicit in human social arrangements.

Reason in Religion, Volume III of *The Life of Reason.* New York: Charles Scribner's Sons, 1905. Attempts to indicate the elements of reason in superstition, magic, prayer, and myth as well as in certain attitudes and doctrines closely associated with the Judeo-Christian tradition.

Reason in Art, Volume IV of *The Life of Reason.* New York: Charles Scribner's Sons, 1905. An examination of the basis, the rationality, the forms, and the justification, aesthetic, intellectual, and moral, of such arts as music, poetry, and painting. The final chapter is concerned with the relation of art to happiness.

Reason in Science, Volume V of *The Life of Reason.* New York: Charles Scribner's Sons, 1906. Not primarily about science as science is generally understood. The chief topics discussed are the nature of science, history, mechanism, psychology, dialectic, and the development of moral judgment and ethics.

Three Philosophical Poets: Lucretius, Dante, and Goethe. Cambridge: Harvard University Press, 1910. A reflective examination of the philosophic ideas expressed in three fundamentally different poetic styles together with suggestions about the more general relations of poetry and philosophy.

Winds of Doctrine: Studies in Contemporary Opinion. London: J. M. Dent & Sons; New York: Charles Scribner's Sons, 1913. Contains essays on various subjects from the philosophy of Bertrand Russell and Henri Bergson to "modernist" trends in Christianity and "the genteel tradition" in American philosophy.

Egotism in German Philosophy. London: J. M. Dent & Sons; New York: Charles Scribner's Sons, 1916. A work inspired largely by the attempt to account for German aggressiveness by an examination of the metaphysical assumptions of such thinkers as Goethe, Kant, Fichte, Schopenhauer, and Nietzsche.

Character and Opinion in the United States, with Reminiscences of William James and Josiah Royce and Academic Life in America. New York: Charles Scribner's Sons, 1920. Contains critical essays on American academic life, on William James and Josiah Royce, and discussions of the conflict in America between materialism and idealism and of the development of English "Liberty" in a new world.

Soliloquies in England and Later Soliloquies. New York: Charles Scribner's Sons, 1922. Fifty-five short essays, some literary and others philosophical; many of the latter are particularly important as first introductions of the mood, ideas, and directions that characterized his later works. Available in paperback from the University of Michigan Press.

Scepticism and Animal Faith: Introduction to a System of Philosophy. New York: Charles Scribner's Sons, 1923. Intended originally as an introduction to *Realms of Being;* remains perhaps the best single statement of his philosophy, particularly his metaphysics and theory of knowledge; defends the claim that "nothing given exists," that "knowledge is faith mediated by symbols," and that truth is possible only through disillusion. Available in paperback from Dover Publications.

Dialogues in Limbo. New York: Charles Scribner's Sons, 1926 (new edition, including three new dialogues, 1948). Imaginary dialogues with ancient philosophers, particularly Socrates and the materialist, Democritus, on the problems of knowledge and metaphysics.

The Realm of Essence. Book First of Realms of Being. New York: Charles Scribner's Sons, 1927. A systematic development of the theory of essence as the object of all thought, experience, and imagination together with helpful comparisons with similar "doctrines" held by other philosophers.

Platonism and the Spiritual Life. New York: Charles Scribner's Sons, 1927. A short discussion of Platonism in the intellectual or "spiritual" life of Western man. Anticipates in certain respects *The Realm of Spirit* and continues themes from *The Realm of Essence.*

The Realm of Matter. Book Second of Realms of Being. New York: Charles Scribner's Sons, 1930. Defends and develops the claim that "matter" is the primal substance and the matrix of all existence. Also contains his most systematic treatment of teleology and an important chapter on "The Psyche."

The Genteel Tradition at Bay. New York: Charles Scribner's Sons, 1931. Especially the two final chapters of this little book contain perhaps the most precise statement of his appreciation of the moral relevance of Platonism and the "supernatural" while uncompromising in its defense of the moral adequacy of "naturalism."

Some Turns of Thought in Modern Philosophy: Five Essays. New York: Charles Scribner's Sons, 1933. Contains separately written essays on John Locke, British idealism, the theory of relativity, a treatment of Nirvana suggested by Sigmund Freud's *Beyond the Pleasure Principle,* and some reflections, entitled "The Prestige of the Infinite," on the possible relations of God and the world.

Obiter Scripta, Essays and Reviews. New York: Charles Scribner's Sons, 1936. A collection of critical essays and reviews written from 1902 to 1933. Edited by Justus Buchler and Benjamin Swartz. Contains a useful bibliography of books and articles.

The Realm of Truth. Book Third of Realms of Being. New York: Charles Scribner's Sons, 1938. Truth, conceived as the ideal and nonexistent description of existence, is discussed in relation to such distorted forms of it in human experience and discourse as conventional, dramatic, and moral truth.

The Realm of Spirit. Book Fourth of Realms of Being. New York: Charles Scribner's Sons, 1940. The "consummation," intellectually as well as chronologically, of *Realms of Being,* or even of his philosophical reflections. Found here is his most mature and serious defense of the "spiritual life." Also contains his most sustained discussion of such concepts as freedom, intuition, distraction, and the liberation of the spirit.

The Idea of Christ in the Gospels: or God in Man, a Critical Essay. New York: Charles Scribner's Sons, 1946. Written with such moral and spiritual sympathy for Christian doctrine that many were tempted to regard it as a rejection of naturalism. Yet it is clearly consistent with the interpretation of religion as poetic symbol and moral fable first expressed in *Interpretations of Poetry and Religion.*

Dominations and Powers: Reflections on Liberty, Society and Government. New York: Charles Scribner's Sons, 1950, 1951. This final philosophical work from his own hand, written over a period of many years, is made up of more than a hundred short chapters, all related more or less to social and political theory. Ideas are not developed systematically and the chief value of the book is the elaboration of themes introduced in earlier works.

The Idler and His Works and Other Essays. Edited and with a preface by Daniel Cory. New York: George Braziller, Inc., 1957. A collection of essays, some previously unpublished, written throughout his life. The essays range from reflections on his own life and work to interpretations of various philosophers (Plato, Spinoza, James, Croce) and a little poetic piece on "Immortality."

COLLECTIONS OF THE PHILOSOPHIC WORKS OF GEORGE SANTAYANA

Animal Faith and Spiritual Life. Edited by John Lachs. New York: Appleton-Century-Crofts, 1967. Contains previously unpublished and uncollected essays by Santayana himself together with critical essays by several critics.

Little Essays Drawn from the Writings of George Santayana. Edited with a preface by Logan Pearsall Smith. New York: Charles Scribner's Sons, 1920.

The Philosophy of Santayana. Edited, with an introductory essay, by Irwin Edman. New York: The Modern Library, 1936. An enlarged edition of this work, containing selections from the later writings, was published by Charles Scribner's Sons in 1953.

The Works of George Santayana. New York: Charles Scribner's Sons, 1936–1940. Triton Edition. 15 volumes. Limited to 940 copies.

Essays in Literary Criticism of George Santayana. Selected and edited with an introduction by Irving Singer. New York: Charles Scribner's Sons, 1956.

The Wisdom of George Santayana. Selected and edited by Ira D. Cardiff. New York: Philosophical Library, 1964. Published in 1950 as *Atoms of Thoughts from George Santayana.*

CHIEF LITERARY AND AUTOBIOGRAPHICAL WRITINGS AND THE PUBLISHED LETTERS OF GEORGE SANTAYANA

Sonnets and Other Verses. New York: Stone and Kimbell, 1894. Other editions were issued by the same publisher in 1896 and by Duffield and Company in 1906.

Lucifer: A Theological Tragedy. Chicago and New York: Herbert S. Stone and Co., 1899. Second edition, Cambridge, Mass.: Dunster House, 1924.

A Hermit of Carmel, and Other Poems. New York: Charles Scribner's Sons, 1901. Second edition, London: T. Fisher Unwin, 1907.

Poems: Selected by the Author and Revised. New York: Charles Scribner's Sons, 1923.

The Last Puritan: A Memoir in the Form of a Novel. New York: Charles Scribner's Sons, 1936. Available in a paperback edition.

Persons and Places: The Background of My Life. New York: Charles Scribner's Sons, 1944.

The Middle Span, Volume II of *Persons and Places.* New York: Charles Scribner's Sons, 1945.

My Host the World, Volume III of *Persons and Places.* New York: Charles Scribner's Sons, 1953.

The Poet's Testament: Poems and Two Plays. New York: Charles Scribner's Sons, 1953.

The Letters of George Santayana. Edited with an introduction and commentary by Daniel Cory. New York: Charles Scribner's Sons, 1955.

AN ANNOTATED BIBLIOGRAPHY OF THE MOST IMPORTANT BOOKS ON GEORGE SANTAYANA

ARNETT, WILLARD E. *Santayana and the Sense of Beauty.* Bloomington, Indiana: Indiana University Press, 1955. Midland paperback, 1957. An examination of the influence of aesthetic sensitivity, values, and categories on the other elements of Santayana's thought.

ASHMORE, JEROME. *Santayana, Art, and Aesthetic.* Cleveland: Western Reserve University Press, 1966. A serious—but not always clear or sympathetic—attempt to identify the origins and elements of Santayana's aesthetic doctrines and their relation to the "life of reason."

BUTLER, RICHARD, O. P. *The Mind of Santayana.* Chicago: Henry Regnery Company, 1955. A philosophically unsympathetic attempt to show that the materialism and subjectivism of Santayana's thought results in an utter scepticism that is incompatible with genuine philosophy.

———. *The Life and World of George Santayana.* Chicago: Henry Regnery Company, 1960. Interesting, imaginative, and sometimes obviously inaccurate. Not to be completely trusted for either facts or philosophical interpretation.

CORY, DANIEL. *Santayana: The Later Years: A Portrait with Letters.* New York: George Braziller, 1963. Drawing heavily on letters as well as on his close association with Santayana from 1928 until his death, Cory provides a very interesting and highly valuable "portrait" of the man and the philosopher.

Howgate, George W. *George Santayana.* Philadelphia: University of Pennsylvania Press, 1938. An early work containing an interesting account of Santayana's life and character and valuable studies of him as poet, essayist, and critic.

Kirkwood, M. M. *Santayana: Saint of the Imagination.* Toronto: University of Toronto Press, 1961. This work, which "employs as its basic method extensive quotation from the writing," is "a fair and useful introduction to the life and mind of George Santayana." As the title indicates, the emphasis is on the values he found in the imagination and not on his achievements in philosophical analysis.

Munitz, Milton K. *The Moral Philosophy of Santayana.* New York: Columbia University Press, 1939. This book, with a foreword by Irwin Edman, is a careful examination of Santayana's moral doctrine in relation to such central features of his thought as his naturalism, "the life of reason," and "the spiritual life." Reprinted in 1958 by Humanities Press, Inc.

Munson, Thomas N., S. J. *The Essential Wisdom of George Santayana.* New York and London: Columbia University Press, 1962. The title of this book is *essentially* misleading since it is a notable attempt to show that particularly from the viewpoint of the Catholic tradition in philosophy, Santayana completely failed to attain wisdom. This book is especially valuable for its bibliography of articles by and about Santayana.

Schlipp, Paul Arthur (ed.). *The Philosophy of George Santayana.* Evanston and Chicago: *The Library of Living Philosophers,* 1940, 1951. No doubt the most valuable single volume on Santayana for the serious student of his philosophy. The volume contains appreciative surveys of various aspects of his life and thought, searching critical examination of his claims and arguments, and an introduction and reply to his critics by Santayana himself.

Singer, Irving. *Santayana's Aesthetics: A Critical Introduction.* Cambridge, Mass.: Harvard University Press, 1957. A very careful analysis of the concepts involved in Santayana's aesthetic theory, in his approach to the arts, and in his criteria of criticism; attempts also to indicate what a more adequate theory of aesthetics, the arts, and criticism would demand.

OTHER BOOKS CITED

Dewey, John, *A Common Faith,* New Haven, Yale, 1934.

——— *Art as Experience,* New York, Minton, Balch & Co., 1934.

——— *Essays in Experimental Logic,* New York, Dover, 1953.

——— *Experience and Nature,* London, Allen & Unwin, 1929.

——— *Logic: The Theory of Inquiry,* New York, Henry Holt and Company, 1938.

——— *On Experience, Nature and Freedom,* R. Bernstein, ed., New York, Bobbs-Merrill, 1960.

Fisch, Max H., *Classic American Philosophers,* New York, Appleton-Century-Crofts, 1951.

Husserl, Edmund, *Ideas: General Introduction to a Pure Phenomenology,* London and New York, Allen & Unwin and Macmillan, 1931.

James, William, *Essays in Radical Empiricism,* R. B. Perry, ed., New York, Longmans, Green, & Co., 1912.

——— *A Pluralistic Universe,* New York, Longmans, Green, & Co., 1909.

——— *Pragmatism: A New Name for Some Old Ways of Thinking,* New York, Longmans, Green, & Co., 1907.

——— *The Principles of Psychology,* 2 vols., London, Macmillan, 1905.

——— *The Will To Believe and Other Essays in Popular Philosophy,* New York, Dover, 1956.

Lucretius, *On the Nature of Things,* in *The Stoic and Epicurean Philosophers,* Whitney J. Oates, ed., New York, Random House, 1940.

Mill, J. S., *A System of Logic,* 2 vols., London, Parker, Son, and Bourn West Strand, 1862.

Moore, G. E., *Philosophical Studies,* London, Routledge & Kegan Paul, Ltd., 1922.

Peirce, Charles S., *Philosophical Writings of Peirce,* Justus Buchler, ed., Dover, 1955.

——— *Values in a Universe of Chance,* Philip P. Weiner, ed., Garden City, Doubleday and Co., 1958.

Royce, Josiah, *The Problem of Christianity,* 2 vols., New York, Macmillan, 1913.

——— *The World and the Individual,* 2 vols., New York, Dover, 1959.

Smith, John E., *The Spirit of American Philosophy,* New York, Oxford, 1963.

Thomas, Dylan, *The Collected Poems of Dylan Thomas,* New York, New Directions, 1953.

Wittgenstein, Ludwig, *Tractatus Logico-Philosophicus,* London, Kegan Paul, 1922.

Wright, Chauncey, *Philosophical Writings of Chauncey Wright,* Edward H. Madden, ed., New York, The Liberal Arts Press, 1958.

INDEX